FOURTH AMENDMENT

SEARCH AND SEIZURE

CONTENTS

SEARCH AND SEIZURE

FOURTH AMENDMENT

The right of the people to be secure in their persons, houses, papers, and effects, against unreasonable searches and seizures, shall not be violated, and no Warrants shall issue but upon probable cause, supported by Oath or affirmation, and particularly describing the place to be searched, and the persons or things to be seized.

SEARCH AND SEIZURE

History and Scope of the Amendment

History.—Few provisions of the Bill of Rights grew so directly out of the experience of the colonials as the Fourth Amendment, embodying as it did the protection against the use of the "writs of assistance." But though the insistence on freedom from unreasonable searches and seizures as a fundamental right gained expression in the colonies late and as a result of experience,[1] there was also a rich English experience to draw on. "Every man's house is his castle" was a maxim much celebrated in England, as *Saman's Case* demonstrated in 1603.[2] A civil case of execution of process, *Saman's Case* nonetheless recognized the right of the homeowner to defend his house against unlawful entry even by the King's agents, but at the same time recognized the authority of the appropriate officers to break and enter upon notice in order to arrest or to execute the King's process. Most famous of the English cases was *Entick v. Carrington*,[3] one of a series of civil actions against state officers who, pursuant to general warrants, had raided many homes and other places in search of materials connected with John Wilkes' po-

---

[1] Apparently the first statement of freedom from unreasonable searches and seizures appeared in The Rights of the Colonists and a List of Infringements and Violations of Rights, 1772, in the drafting of which Samuel Adams took the lead. 1 B. SCHWARTZ, THE BILL OF RIGHTS: A DOCUMENTARY HISTORY 199, 205–06 (1971).

[2] 5 Coke's Repts. 91a, 77 Eng. Rep. 194 (K.B. 1604). One of the most forceful expressions of the maxim was that of William Pitt in Parliament in 1763: "The poorest man may in his cottage bid defiance to all the force of the crown. It may be frail—its roof may shake—the wind may blow through it—the storm may enter, the rain may enter—but the King of England cannot enter—all his force dares not cross the threshold of the ruined tenement."

[3] 19 Howell's State Trials 1029, 95 Eng. 807 (1705).

lemical pamphlets attacking not only governmental policies but the King himself.[4]

Entick, an associate of Wilkes, sued because agents had forcibly broken into his house, broken into locked desks and boxes, and seized many printed charts, pamphlets, and the like. In an opinion sweeping in terms, the court declared the warrant and the behavior it authorized subversive "of all the comforts of society," and the issuance of a warrant for the seizure of all of a person's papers rather than only those alleged to be criminal in nature "contrary to the genius of the law of England."[5] Besides its general character, the court said, the warrant was bad because it was not issued on a showing of probable cause and no record was required to be made of what had been seized. *Entick v. Carrington*, the Supreme Court has said, is a "great judgment," "one of the landmarks of English liberty," "one of the permanent monuments of the British Constitution," and a guide to an understanding of what the Framers meant in writing the Fourth Amendment.[6]

In the colonies, smuggling rather than seditious libel afforded the leading examples of the necessity for protection against unreasonable searches and seizures. In order to enforce the revenue laws, English authorities made use of writs of assistance, which were general warrants authorizing the bearer to enter any house or other place to search for and seize "prohibited and uncustomed" goods, and commanding all subjects to assist in these endeavors. Once issued, the writs remained in force throughout the lifetime of the sovereign and six months thereafter. When, upon the death of George II in 1760, the authorities were required to obtain the issuance of new writs, opposition was led by James Otis, who attacked such writs on libertarian grounds and who asserted the invalidity of the authorizing statutes because they conflicted with English constitutionalism.[7] Otis lost and the writs were issued and used, but his arguments were much cited in the colonies not only on the immediate subject but also with regard to judicial review.

Scope of the Amendment.—The language of the provision that became the Fourth Amendment underwent some modest changes

---

[4] *See also* Wilkes v. Wood, 98 Eng. 489 (C.P. 1763); Huckle v. Money, 95 Eng. Rep. 768 (K.B. 1763), *aff'd* 19 Howell's State Trials 1002, 1028; 97 Eng. Rep. 1075 (K.B. 1765).

[5] 95 Eng. 817, 818.

[6] Boyd v. United States, 116 U.S. 616, 626 (1886).

[7] The arguments of Otis and others as well as much background material are contained in Quincy's Massachusetts Reports, 1761–1772, App. I, pp. 395–540, and in 2 Legal Papers of John Adams 106–47 (Wroth & Zobel eds., 1965). *See also* Dickerson, *Writs of Assistance as a Cause of the American Revolution*, in The Era of the American Revolution: Studies Inscribed to Evarts Boutell Greene 40 (R. Morris, ed., 1939).

on its passage through the Congress, and it is possible that the changes reflected more than a modest significance in the interpretation of the relationship of the two clauses. Madison's introduced version provided "The rights to be secured in their persons, their houses, their papers, and their other property, from all unreasonable searches and seizures, shall not be violated by warrants issued without probable cause, supported by oath or affirmation, or not particularly describing the places to be searched, or the persons or things to be seized." [8] As reported from committee, with an inadvertent omission corrected on the floor,[9] the section was almost identical to the introduced version, and the House defeated a motion to substitute "and no warrant shall issue" for "by warrants issuing" in the committee draft. In some fashion, the rejected amendment was inserted in the language before passage by the House and is the language of the ratified constitutional provision.[10]

As noted above, the noteworthy disputes over search and seizure in England and the colonies revolved about the character of warrants. There were, however, lawful warrantless searches, primarily searches incident to arrest, and these apparently gave rise to no disputes. Thus, the question arises whether the Fourth Amendment's two clauses must be read together to mean that the only searches and seizures which are "reasonable" are those which meet the requirements of the second clause, that is, are pursuant to warrants issued under the prescribed safeguards, or whether the two clauses are independent, so that searches under warrant must comply with the second clause but that there are "reasonable" searches under the first clause that need not comply with the second clause.[11] This issue has divided the Court for some time, has seen several reversals of precedents, and is important for the resolution of many

---

[8] 1 ANNALS OF CONGRESS 434–35 (June 8, 1789).

[9] The word "secured" was changed to "secure" and the phrase "against unreasonable searches and seizures" was reinstated. Id. at 754 (August 17, 1789).

[10] Id. It has been theorized that the author of the defeated revision, who was chairman of the committee appointed to arrange the amendments prior to House passage, simply inserted his provision and that it passed unnoticed. N. LASSON, THE HISTORY AND DEVELOPMENT OF THE FOURTH AMENDMENT TO THE UNITED STATES CONSTITUTION 101–03 (1937).

[11] The amendment was originally in one clause as quoted above; it was the insertion of the defeated amendment to the language which changed the text into two clauses and arguably had the effect of extending the protection against unreasonable searches and seizures beyond the requirements imposed on the issuance of warrants. It is also possible to read the two clauses together to mean that some seizures even under warrants would be unreasonable, and this reading has indeed been effectuated in certain cases, although for independent reasons. Boyd v. United States, 116 U.S. 616 (1886); Gouled v. United States, 255 U.S. 298 (1921), overruled by Warden v. Hayden, 387 U.S. 294 (1967); but see id. at 303 (reserving the question whether "there are items of evidential value whose very nature precludes them from being the object of a reasonable search and seizure.")

cases. It is a dispute that has run most consistently throughout the cases involving the scope of the right to search incident to arrest.[12] Although the right to search the person of the arrestee without a warrant is unquestioned, how far afield into areas within and without the control of the arrestee a search may range is an interesting and crucial matter.

The Court has drawn a wavering line.[13] In *Harris v. United States*,[14] it approved as "reasonable" the warrantless search of a four-room apartment pursuant to the arrest of the man found there. A year later, however, a reconstituted Court majority set aside a conviction based on evidence seized by a warrantless search pursuant to an arrest and adopted the "cardinal rule that, in seizing goods and articles, law enforcement agents must secure and use search warrants wherever reasonably practicable."[15] This rule was set aside two years later by another reconstituted majority, which adopted the premise that the test "is not whether it is reasonable to procure a search warrant, but whether the search was reasonable." Whether a search is reasonable, the Court said, "must find resolution in the facts and circumstances of each case."[16] However, the Court soon returned to its emphasis upon the warrant. "The [Fourth] Amendment was in large part a reaction to the general warrants and warrantless searches that had so alienated the colonists and had helped speed the movement for independence. In the scheme of the Amendment, therefore, the requirement that 'no Warrants shall issue, but upon probable cause,' plays a crucial part."[17] Therefore, "the police must, whenever practicable, obtain advance judicial approval of searches and seizures through a warrant procedure."[18] Exceptions to searches under warrants were to be closely

---

[12] Approval of warrantless searches pursuant to arrest first appeared in dicta in several cases. Weeks v. United States, 232 U.S. 383, 392 (1914); Carroll v. United States, 267 U.S. 132, 158 (1925); Agnello v. United States, 269 U.S. 20, 30 (1925). Whether or not there is to be a rule or a principle generally preferring or requiring searches pursuant to warrant to warrantless searches, however, has ramifications far beyond the issue of searches pursuant to arrest. United States v. United States District Court, 407 U.S. 297, 320 (1972).

[13] *Compare* Marron v. United States, 275 U.S. 192 (1927), *with* Go-Bart Importing Co. v. United States, 282 U.S. 344 (1931), *and* United States v. Lefkowitz, 285 U.S. 452 (1932).

[14] 331 U.S. 145 (1947).

[15] Trupiano v. United States, 334 U.S. 699, 705 (1948). *See also* McDonald v. United States, 335 U.S. 451 (1948).

[16] United States v. Rabinowitz, 339 U.S. 56, 66 (1950).

[17] Chimel v. California, 395 U.S. 752, 761 (1969).

[18] Terry v. Ohio, 392 U.S. 1, 20 (1968). In United States v. United States District Court, 407 U.S. 297, 321 (1972), Justice Powell explained that the "very heart" of the Amendment's mandate is "that where practical, a governmental search and seizure should represent both the efforts of the officer to gather evidence of wrongful acts and the judgment of the magistrate that the collected evidence is sufficient

contained by the rationale undergirding the necessity for the exception, and the scope of a search under one of the exceptions was similarly limited.[19]

During the 1970s the Court was closely divided on which standard to apply.[20] For a while, the balance tipped in favor of the view that warrantless searches are *per se* unreasonable, with a few carefully prescribed exceptions.[21] Gradually, guided by the variable-expectation-of-privacy approach to coverage of the Fourth Amendment, the Court broadened its view of permissible exceptions and of the scope of those exceptions.[22] By 1992, it was no longer the case that the "warrants-with-narrow-exceptions" standard nor-

to justify invasion of a citizen's private premises or conversation." Thus, what is "reasonable" in terms of a search and seizure derives content and meaning through reference to the warrant clause. Coolidge v. New Hampshire, 403 U.S. 443, 473–84 (1971). *See also* Davis v. Mississippi, 394 U.S. 721, 728 (1969); Katz v. United States, 389 U.S. 347, 356–58 (1967); Warden v. Hayden, 387 U.S. 294, 299 (1967).

[19] Chimel v. California, 395 U.S. 752, 762–64 (1969) (limiting scope of search incident to arrest). *See also* United States v. United States District Court, 407 U.S. 297 (1972) (rejecting argument that it was "reasonable" to allow President through Attorney General to authorize warrantless electronic surveillance of persons thought to be endangering the national security); Katz v. United States, 389 U.S. 347 (1967) (although officers acted with great self-restraint and reasonably in engaging in electronic seizures of conversations from a telephone booth, a magistrate's antecedent judgment was required); Preston v. United States, 376 U.S. 364 (1964) (warrantless search of seized automobile not justified because not within rationale of exceptions to warrant clause). There were exceptions, *e.g.*, Cooper v. California, 386 U.S. 58 (1967) (warrantless search of impounded car was reasonable); United States v. Harris, 390 U.S. 234 (1968) (warrantless inventory search of automobile).

[20] *See, e.g.*, Almighty-Sanchez v. United States, 413 U.S. 266 (1973), Justices Stewart, Douglas, Brennan, and Marshall adhered to the warrant-based rule, while Justices White, Blackmun, and Rehnquist, and Chief Justice Burger placed greater emphasis upon the question of reasonableness without necessary regard to the warrant requirement. Id. at 285. Justice Powell generally agreed with the former group of Justices, id. at 275 (concurring).

[21] *E.g.*, G.M. Leasing Corp. v. United States, 429 U.S. 338, 352–53 (1977) (unanimous); Marshall v. Barrow's, Inc., 436 U.S. 307, 312 (1978); Michigan v. Tyler, 436 U.S. 499, 506 (1978); Mincey v. Arizona, 437 U.S. 385, 390 (1978) (unanimous); Arkansas v. Sanders, 442 U.S. 743 (1979) (1979); United States v. Ross, 456 U.S. 798, 824–25 (1982).

[22] *E.g.*, Chambers v. Maroney, 399 U.S. 42 (1970) (warrantless search of automobile taken to police station); Texas v. White, 423 U.S. 67 (1975) (same); New York v. Belton, 453 U.S. 454 (1981) (search of vehicle incident to arrest); United States v. Ross, 456 U.S. 798 (1982) (automobile search at scene); Brigham City, Utah v. Stuart, 547 U.S. 398 (2006) (warrantless entry into a home when police have an objectively reasonable basis for believing that an occupant is seriously injured or imminently threatened with such injury); Michigan v. Fisher, 558 U.S. ___, No. 09–91 (2009) (applying *Brigham City*). On the other hand, the warrant-based standard did preclude a number of warrantless searches. *E.g.*, Almighty-Sanchez v. United States, 413 U.S. 266 (1973) (warrantless stop and search of auto by roving patrol near border); Marshall v. Barrow's, Inc., 436 U.S. 307 (1978) (warrantless administrative inspection of business premises); Mincey v. Arizona, 437 U.S. 385 (1978) (warrantless search of home that was "homicide scene"); Arizona v. Gant, 556 U.S. ___, No. 07–542 (2009) (search of vehicle incident to arrest where arrestee had no access to vehicle).

mally prevails over a "reasonableness" approach.[23] Exceptions to the warrant requirement have multiplied, tending to confine application of the requirement to cases that are exclusively "criminal" in nature. And even within that core area of "criminal" cases, some exceptions have been broadened.

The most important category of exception is that of administrative searches justified by "special needs beyond the normal need for law enforcement." Under this general rubric the Court has upheld warrantless searches by administrative authorities in public schools, government offices, and prisons, and has upheld drug testing of public and transportation employees.[24] In all of these instances, the warrant and probable cause requirements are dispensed with in favor of a reasonableness standard that balances the government's regulatory interest against the individual's privacy interest; in all of these instances, the government's interest has been found to outweigh the individual's. The broad scope of the administrative search exception is evidenced by the fact that an overlap between law enforcement objectives and administrative "special needs" does not result in application of the warrant requirement; instead, the Court has upheld warrantless inspection of automobile junkyards and dismantling operations in spite of the strong law enforcement component of the regulation.[25]

In the law enforcement context, where search by warrant is still the general rule, there has also been some loosening of the requirement. For example, the scope of a valid search "incident to arrest," once limited to areas within the immediate reach of the arrested suspect, was expanded to a "protective sweep" of the entire home, if arresting officers have a "reasonable" belief that the home harbors an individual who may pose a danger.[26] In another case, the Court shifted focus from whether exigent circumstances justified failure to obtain a warrant, to whether an officer had a "reasonable" belief that an exception to the warrant requirement applied.[27] The Court has also held that an exigent circumstances exception ap-

---

[23] Of the Justices on the Court in 1992, only Justice Stevens frequently sided with the warrants-with-narrow-exceptions approach. *See, e.g.,* Illinois v. Rodriguez, 497 U.S. 177, 189 (Justice Stevens joining Justice Marshall's dissent); New Jersey v. T.L.O., 469 U.S. 325, 370 (1985) (Justice Stevens dissenting); California v. Acevedo, 500 U.S. 565, 585 (1991) (Justice Stevens dissenting).

[24] *See* various headings *infra* under the general heading "Valid Searches and Seizures Without Warrants."

[25] New York v. Burger, 482 U.S. 691 (1987).

[26] Maryland v. Buie, 494 U.S. 325 (1990).

[27] Illinois v. Rodriguez, 497 U.S. 177 (1990); *see also* Missouri v. McNeely, 569 U.S. ___, No. 11–1425, slip op. (2013) (rejecting a per se exception for obtaining warrants in DWI cases and requiring that exigent circumstances be evaluated under a "totality of the circumstances" test).

plied even where the exigency arose as a result of police conduct, so long as the police conduct was "reasonable" in that it neither threatened to nor violated the Fourth Amendment.[28]

Another matter of scope that the Court has addressed is the category of persons protected by the Fourth Amendment; *i.e.*, who constitutes "the people." This phrase, the Court determined, "refers to a class of persons who are part of a national community or who have otherwise developed sufficient connection with [the United States] to be considered part of that community."[29] The Fourth Amendment therefore does not apply to the search and seizure by United States agents of property that is owned by a nonresident alien and located in a foreign country. The community of protected people includes U.S. citizens who go abroad, and aliens who have voluntarily entered U.S. territory and developed substantial connections with this country. There is no resulting broad principle, however, that the Fourth Amendment constrains federal officials wherever and against whomever they act.

The Interest Protected.—For the Fourth Amendment to apply to a particular set of facts, there must be a "search" and a "seizure," occurring typically in a criminal case, with a subsequent attempt to use judicially what was seized.[30] Whether there was a search and seizure within the meaning of the Amendment, and whether a complainant's interests were constitutionally infringed, will often turn upon consideration of his interest and whether it was officially abused. What does the Amendment protect? Under the common law, there was no doubt. In *Entick v. Carrington*,[31] Lord Camden wrote: "The great end for which men entered in society was to secure their property. That right is preserved sacred and incommunicable in all instances where it has not been taken away or abridged by some public law for the good of the whole. . . . By the laws of England, every invasion of private property, be it ever so minute, is a trespass. No man can set foot upon my ground without my license but he is liable to an action though the damage be nothing . . . ." Protection of property interests as the basis of the Fourth Amendment found

---

[28] Kentucky v. King, 563 U.S. ___, No. 09–1272, slip op. (2011) (police justified in entering apartment after smelling burning marijuana in a hallway, knocking on apartment door, and hearing noises consistent with evidence being destroyed).

[29] United States v. Vertigo-Urquidez, 494 U.S. 259, 265 (1990).

[30] *See, e.g.*, California v. Hodari D., 499 U.S. 621, 626 (1991) (because there was no "seizure" of the defendant as he fled from police before being tackled, the drugs that he abandoned in flight could not be excluded as the fruits of an unreasonable seizure).

[31] 19 Howell's State Trials 1029, 1035, 95 Eng. Reg. 807, 817–18 (1765).

easy acceptance in the Supreme Court [32] and that acceptance controlled the decision in numerous cases.[33] For example, in *Olmstead v. United States*,[34] one of the two premises underlying the holding that wiretapping was not covered by the Amendment was that there had been no actual physical invasion of the defendant's premises; where there had been an invasion—a technical trespass—electronic surveillance was deemed subject to Fourth Amendment restrictions.[35]

The Court later rejected this approach. "The premise that property interests control the right of the government to search and seize has been discredited. . . . We have recognized that the principal object of the Fourth Amendment is the protection of privacy rather than property, and have increasingly discarded fictional and procedural barriers rested on property concepts." [36] Thus, because the Amendment "protects people, not places," the requirement of actual physical trespass is dispensed with and electronic surveillance was made subject to the Amendment's requirements.[37]

The new test, propounded in *Katz v. United States*, is whether there is an expectation of privacy upon which one may "justifiably" rely.[38] "What a person knowingly exposes to the public, even in his own home or office, is not a subject of Fourth Amendment protection. But what he seeks to preserve as private, even in an area ac-

---

[32] Boyd v. United States, 116 U.S. 616, 627 (1886); Adams v. New York, 192 U.S. 585, 598 (1904).

[33] Thus, the rule that "mere evidence" could not be seized but rather only the fruits of crime, its instrumentalities, or contraband, turned upon the question of the right of the public to possess the materials or the police power to make possession by the possessor unlawful. Gouled v. United States, 255 U.S. 298 (1921), overruled by Warden v. Hayden, 387 U.S. 294 (1967). *See also* Davis v. United States, 328 U.S. 582 (1946). Standing to contest unlawful searches and seizures was based upon property interests, United States v. Jeffers, 342 U.S. 48 (1951); Jones v. United States, 362 U.S. 257 (1960), as well as decision upon the validity of a consent to search. Chapman v. United States, 365 U.S. 610 (1961); Stoner v. California, 376 U.S. 483 (1964); Frazier v. Culp, 394 U.S. 731, 740 (1969).

[34] 277 U.S. 438 (1928). *See also* Goldman v. United States, 316 U.S. 129 (1942) (detectaphone placed against wall of adjoining room; no search and seizure).

[35] Silverman v. United States, 365 U.S. 505 (1961) (spike mike pushed through a party wall until it hit a heating duct).

[36] Warden v. Hayden, 387 U.S. 294, 304 (1967).

[37] Katz v. United States, 389 U.S. 347, 353 (1967) (warrantless use of listening and recording device placed on outside of phone booth violates Fourth Amendment). *See also* Kyllo v. United States, 533 U.S. 27, 32–33 (2001) (holding presumptively unreasonable the warrantless use of a thermal imaging device to detect activity within a home by measuring heat outside the home, and noting that a contrary holding would permit developments in police technology "to erode the privacy guaranteed by the Fourth Amendment".

[38] 389 U.S. at 353. Justice Harlan, concurring, formulated a two pronged test for determining whether the privacy interest is paramount: "first that a person have exhibited an actual (subjective) expectation of privacy and, second, that the expectation be one that society is prepared to recognize as 'reasonable.'" Id. at 361.

cessible to the public, may be constitutionally protected."[39] That is, the "capacity to claim the protection of the Amendment depends not upon a property right in the invaded place but upon whether the area was one in which there was reasonable expectation of freedom from governmental intrusion."[40]

Katz's focus on privacy was revitalized in *Kyllo v. United States*,[41] in which the Court invalidated the warrantless use of a thermal imaging device directed at a private home from a public street. The rule devised by the Court to limit police use of new technology that can "shrink the realm of guaranteed privacy" is that "obtaining by sense-enhancing technology any information regarding the interior of the home that could not otherwise have been obtained without physical 'intrusion into a constitutionally protected area' . . . constitutes a search—at least where (as here) the technology in question is not in general public use."[42] Relying on *Katz*, the Court rejected as "mechanical" the Government's attempted distinction between off-the-wall and through-the-wall surveillance. Permitting all off-the-wall observations, the Court observed, "would leave the homeowner at the mercy of advancing technology—including technology that could discern all human activity in the home."

Although the sanctity of the home has been strongly reaffirmed, protection of privacy in other contexts becomes more problematic. A two-part test that Justice Harlan suggested in *Katz* often provides the starting point for analysis.[43] The first element, the

---

[39] 389 U.S. at 351–52.

[40] Mancusi v. DeForte, 392 U.S. 364, 368 (1968) (official had a reasonable expectation of privacy in an office he shared with others, although he owned neither the premises nor the papers seized). Minnesota v. Olson, 495 U.S. 91 (1990) (overnight guest in home has a reasonable expectation of privacy). *But cf.* Minnesota v. Carter, 525 U.S. 83 (1998) (a person present in someone else's apartment for only a few hours for the purpose of bagging cocaine for later sale has no legitimate expectation of privacy); *Cf.* Rakas v. Illinois, 439 U.S. 128 (1978) (auto passengers demonstrated no legitimate expectation of privacy in glove compartment or under seat of auto). Property rights are still protected by the Amendment, however. A "seizure" of property can occur when there is some meaningful interference with an individual's possessory interests in that property, and regardless of whether there is any interference with the individual's privacy interest. Soldal v. Cook County, 506 U.S. 56 (1992) (a seizure occurred when sheriff's deputies assisted in the disconnection and removal of a mobile home in the course of an eviction from a mobile home park). The reasonableness of a seizure, however, is an additional issue that may still hinge on privacy interests. United States v. Jacobsen, 466 U.S. 109, 120–21 (1984) (DEA agents reasonably seized package for examination after private mail carrier had opened the damaged package for inspection, discovered presence of contraband, and informed agents).

[41] 533 U.S. 27 (2001).

[42] 533 U.S. at 34.

[43] Justice Harlan's opinion has been much relied upon. *See, e.g.,* Terry v. Ohio, 392 U.S. 1, 19 (1968); Rakas v. Illinois, 439 U.S. 128, 143–144 n.12 (1978); Smith v. Maryland, 442 U.S. 735, 740–41 (1979); United States v. Salvucci, 448 U.S. 83, 91–92

"subjective expectation" of privacy, has largely dwindled as a viable standard, because, as Justice Harlan noted in a subsequent case, "our expectations, and the risks we assume, are in large part reflections of laws that translate into rules the customs and values of the past and present." [44] As for the second element, whether one has a "legitimate" expectation of privacy that society finds "reasonable" to recognize, the Court has said that "[l]egitimation of expectations of privacy by law must have a source outside of the Fourth Amendment, either by reference to concepts of real or personal property law or to understandings that are recognized and permitted by society." [45]

Thus, protection of the home is at the apex of Fourth Amendment coverage because of the right associated with ownership to exclude others; [46] but ownership of other things, *i.e.*, automobiles, does not carry a similar high degree of protection.[47] That a person has taken normal precautions to maintain his privacy, that is, precautions customarily taken by those seeking to exclude others, is usually a significant factor in determining legitimacy of expectation.[48] Some expectations, the Court has held, are simply not among those that society is prepared to accept.[49] In the context of norms for the use of rapidly evolving communications devices, the Court was reluctant to consider "the whole concept of privacy expectations" at all, preferring other decisional grounds: "The judiciary risks

(1980); Rawlings v. Kentucky, 448 U.S. 98, 105–06 (1980); Bond v. United States, 529 U.S. 334, 338 (2000).

[44] United States v. White, 401 U.S. 745, 786 (1971). *See* Smith v. Maryland, 442 U.S. 735, 740 n.5 (1979) (government could not condition "subjective expectations" by, say, announcing that henceforth all homes would be subject to warrantless entry, and thus destroy the "legitimate expectation of privacy").

[45] Rakas v. Illinois, 439 U.S. 128, 144 n.12 (1978).

[46] *E.g.*, Alderman v. United States, 394 U.S. 165 (1969); Mincey v. Arizona, 437 U.S. 385 (1978); Payton v. New York, 445 U.S. 573 (1980); Kyllo v. United States, 533 U.S. 27, 31 (2001).

[47] *E.g.*, United States v. Ross, 456 U.S. 798 (1982). *See also* Donovan v. Dewey, 452 U.S. 594 (1981) (commercial premises); Maryland v. Macon, 472 U.S. 463 (1985) (no legitimate expectation of privacy in denying to undercover officers allegedly obscene materials offered to public in bookstore).

[48] *E.g.*, United States v. Chadwick, 433 U.S. 1, 11 (1977); Katz v. United States, 389 U.S. 347, 352 (1967). *But cf.* South Dakota v. Opperman, 428 U.S. 364 (1976) (no legitimate expectation of privacy in automobile left with doors locked and windows rolled up). In Rawlings v. Kentucky, 448 U.S. 98 (1980), the fact that defendant had dumped a cache of drugs into his companion's purse, having known her for only a few days and knowing others had access to the purse, was taken to establish that he had no legitimate expectation the purse would be free from intrusion.

[49] *E.g.*, United States v. Miller, 425 U.S. 435 (1976) (bank records); Smith v. Maryland, 442 U.S. 735 (1979) (numbers dialed from one's telephone); Hudson v. Palmer, 468 U.S. 517 (1984) (prison cell); Illinois v. Andreas, 463 U.S. 765 (1983) (shipping container opened and inspected by customs agents and resealed and delivered to the addressee); California v. Greenwood, 486 U.S. 35 (1988) (garbage in sealed plastic bags left at curb for collection).

error by elaborating too fully on the Fourth Amendment implications of emerging technology before its role in society has become clear." [50]

What seems to have emerged is a balancing standard that requires "an assessing of the nature of a particular practice and the likely extent of its impact on the individual's sense of security balanced against the utility of the conduct as a technique of law enforcement." Whereas Justice Harlan saw a greater need to restrain police officers through the warrant requirement as the intrusions on individual privacy grow more extensive,[51] the Court's solicitude for law enforcement objectives frequently tilts the balance in the other direction.

Application of this balancing test, because of the Court's weighing of law enforcement investigative needs,[52] and its subjective evaluation of privacy needs, has led to the creation of a two-tier or sliding-tier scale of privacy interests. The privacy test was originally designed to permit a determination that an interest protected by the Fourth Amendment had been invaded.[53] If it had been, then ordinarily a warrant was required, subject only to the narrowly defined exceptions, and the scope of the search under those exceptions was "strictly tied to and justified by the circumstances which rendered its initiation permissible." [54] But the Court now uses the test to determine whether the interest invaded is important or persuasive enough so that a warrant is required to justify it;[55] if the individual has a lesser expectation of privacy, then the invasion may be justified, absent a warrant, by the reasonableness of the intrusion.[56] Exceptions to the warrant requirement are no longer evaluated solely by

---

[50] City of Ontario v. Quon, 560 U.S. ___, No. 08–1332, slip op. at 10 (2010) The Court cautioned that "[a] broad holding concerning employees' privacy expectations vis-a-vis employer-provided technological equipment might have implications for future cases that cannot be predicted." Id. at 11–12.

[51] United States v. White, 401 U.S. 745, 786–87 (1971) (Justice Harlan dissenting).

[52] E.g., Robbins v. California, 453 U.S. 420, 429, 433–34 (1981) (Justice Powell concurring), quoted with approval in United States v. Ross, 456 U.S. 798, 815–16 & n.21 (1982).

[53] Katz v. United States, 389 U.S. 347, 351–52 (1967).

[54] Terry v. Ohio, 392 U.S. 1, 19 (1968).

[55] The prime example is the home, so that for entries either to search or to arrest, "the Fourth Amendment has drawn a firm line at the entrance to the house. Absent exigent circumstances, that threshold may not reasonably be crossed without a warrant." Payton v. New York, 445 U.S. 573, 590 (1980); Steagald v. United States, 451 U.S. 204, 212 (1981); Kirk v. Louisiana, 536 U.S. 635 (2002) (per curiam). See also Mincey v. Arizona, 437 U.S. 385 (1978). Privacy in the home is not limited to intimate matters. "In the home all details are intimate details, because the entire area is held safe from prying government eyes." Kyllo v. United States, 533 U.S. 27, 37 (2001).

[56] One has a diminished expectation of privacy in automobiles. Arkansas v. Sanders, 442 U.S. 753, 761 (1979) (collecting cases); United States v. Ross, 456 U.S. 798,

the justifications for the exception, *e.g.*, exigent circumstances, and the scope of the search is no longer tied to and limited by the justification for the exception.[57] The result has been a considerable expansion, beyond what existed prior to *Katz*, of the power of police and other authorities to conduct searches.

In *United States v. Jones*,[58] the Court seemed to revitalize the significance of governmental trespass in determining whether a Fourth Amendment search has occurred. In *Jones*, the Court considered whether the attachment of a Global-Positioning-System (GPS) device to a car used by a suspected narcotics dealer and the monitoring of such device for twenty-eight days, constituted a search. Although the Court ruled unanimously that this month-long monitoring violated Jones's rights, it splintered on the reasoning. A majority of the Court relied on the theory of common law trespass to find that the attachment of the device to the car represented a physical intrusion into Jones's constitutionally protected "effect" or private property.[59] While this holding obviated the need to assess the month-

804–09 (1982). A person's expectation of privacy in personal luggage and other closed containers is substantially greater than in an automobile, United States v. Chadwick, 433 U.S. 1, 13 (1977); Arkansas v. Sanders, 442 U.S. 753 (1979), although, if the luggage or container is found in an automobile as to which there exists probable cause to search, the legitimate expectancy diminishes accordingly. United States v. Ross, *supra*. There is also a diminished expectation of privacy in a mobile home parked in a parking lot and licensed for vehicular travel. California v. Carney, 471 U.S. 386 (1985) (leaving open the question of whether the automobile exception also applies to a "mobile" home being used as a residence and not adapted for immediate vehicular use).

[57] *E.g.*, Texas v. White, 423 U.S. 67 (1975) (if probable cause to search automobile existed at scene, it can be removed to station and searched without warrant); United States v. Robinson, 414 U.S. 218 (1973) (once an arrest has been validly made, search pursuant thereto is so minimally intrusive in addition that scope of search is not limited by necessity of security of officer); United States v. Edwards, 415 U.S. 800 (1974) (incarcerated suspect; officers need no warrant to take his clothes for test because little additional intrusion). *But see* Ybarra v. Illinois, 444 U.S. 85 (1979) (officers on premises to execute search warrant of premises may not without more search persons found on premises).

[58] 565 U.S. ___, No. 10–1259, slip op. (2012).

[59] *Id.* at 3–7. The physical trespass analysis was reprised in subsequent opinions. In its 2013 decision in *Florida v. Jardines*, the Court assessed whether a law enforcement officer had the legal authority to conduct a drug sniff with a trained canine on the front porch of a suspect's home. Reviewing the law of trespass, the Court observed that visitors to a home, including the police, must have either explicit or implicit authority from the homeowner to enter upon and engage in various activities in the curtilage (i.e., the area immediately surrounding the home). Finding that the use of the dog to find incriminating evidence exceeded "background social norms" of what a visitor is normally permitted to do on another's property, the Court held that the drug sniff constituted a search. 569 U.S. ___, No. 11–564, slip op. at 5–8 (2013). Similarly, in its 2015 per curiam opinion in *Grady v. North Carolina*, the Court emphasized the "physical intru[sion]" on a person when it found that attaching a device to a person's body, without consent, for the purpose of tracking the person's movements, constitutes a search within the meaning of the Fourth Amendment. 575 U.S. ___, No. 14–593, slip op. at 4–5 (2015). Neither the majority in *Jardines*

long tracking under *Katz*'s reasonable expectation of privacy test, five Justices, who concurred either with the majority opinion or concurred with the judgment, would have held that long-term GPS tracking can implicate an individual's expectation of privacy.[60] Some have read these concurrences as partly premised on the idea that while government access to a small data set—for example, one trip in a vehicle—might not violate one's expectation of privacy, aggregating a month's worth of personal data allows the government to create a "mosaic" about an individual's personal life that violates that individual's reasonable expectation of privacy.[61] As a consequence, these concurring opinions could potentially have significant implications for the scope of the Fourth Amendment in relation to current and future technologies, such as cell phone tracking and wearable technologies that do not require a physical trespass to monitor a person's activities and that can aggregate a wealth of personal data about users.[62]

Arrests and Other Detentions.—That the Fourth Amendment was intended to protect against arbitrary arrests as well as against unreasonable searches was early assumed by Chief Justice Marshall[63] and is now established law.[64] At common law, warrant-

---

nor the Court in *Grady* addressed whether the challenged conduct violates a reasonable expectation of privacy under *Katz v. United States*. *Grady*, slip op. at 5; *Jardines*, slip op. at 8–10.

[60] *Jones*, slip op. at 14 (Alito, J., concurring in the judgment, joined by Ginsburg, Breyer, Kagan, JJ.) (concluding that respondent's reasonable expectations of privacy were violated by the long-term monitoring of the movements of the respondent's vehicle); *id.* at 3 (Sotomayor, J., concurring) (disagreeing with Justice Alito's "approach" to the specific case but agreeing "longer term GPS monitoring in investigations of most offenses impinges on expectations of privacy.").

[61] *See, e.g.*, United States v. Graham, 846 F.Supp. 2d 384, 394 (D. Md. 2012) ("It appears as though a five-Justice majority is willing to accept the principle that government surveillance over time can implicate an individual's reasonable expectation of privacy."), *aff'd*, ___ F.3d ___, No. 12–4659, slip op. at 31 (4th Cir. 2015); *In re* Application for Telephone Information Needed for a Criminal Investigation, 119 F. Supp. 3d. 1011, 1021–22 (N.D. Cal. 2015) (discussing the import of the two concurring opinions from *Jones*); United States v. Brooks, 911 F. Supp. 2d 836, 842 (D. Ariz. 2012) (noting that "[w]hile it does appear that in some future case, a five justice 'majority' is willing to accept the principle that Government surveillance can implicate an individual's reasonable expectation of privacy over time, *Jones* does not dictate the result of the case at hand . . . "); *but see* United States v. Graham, ___ F.3d ___, No. 12–4659, 2016 WL 3068018, at *10 (4th Cir. May 31, 2016) (arguing that Justice Alito's *Jones* concurrence should be read more narrowly so as to not implicate government access to information collected by third-party actors, no matter the quantity of information collected); *In re* Application of FBI, No. BR 14–01, 2014 WL 5463097, at *10 (FISA Ct. Mar. 20, 2014) ("While the concurring opinions in *Jones* may signal that some or even most of the Justices are ready to revisit certain settled Fourth Amendment principles, the decision in *Jones* itself breaks no new ground . . .").

[62] *See generally* Orin S. Kerr, *The Mosaic Theory of the Fourth Amendment*, 111 MICH. L. REV. 311 (2012).

[63] *Ex parte* Burford, 7 U.S. (3 Cr.) 448 (1806).

less arrests of persons who had committed a breach of the peace or a felony were permitted,[65] and this history is reflected in the fact that the Fourth Amendment is satisfied if the arrest is made in a public place on probable cause, regardless of whether a warrant has been obtained.[66] However, in order to effectuate an arrest in the home, absent consent or exigent circumstances, police officers must have a warrant.[67]

The Fourth Amendment applies to "seizures" and it is not necessary that a detention be a formal arrest in order to bring to bear the requirements of warrants, or probable cause in instances in which warrants are not required.[68] Some objective justification must be shown to validate all seizures of the person,[69] including seizures

---

[64] Giordenello v. United States, 357 U.S. 480, 485–86 (1958); United States v. Watson, 423 U.S. 411, 416–18 (1976); Payton v. New York, 445 U.S. 573, 583–86 (1980); Steagald v. United States, 451 U.S. 204, 211–13 (1981).

[65] 1 J. STEPHEN, A HISTORY OF THE CRIMINAL LAW OF ENGLAND 193 (1883). At common law warrantless arrest was also permissible for some misdemeanors not involving a breach of the peace. See the lengthy historical treatment in Atwater v. City of Lago Vista, 532 U.S. 318, 326–45 (2001).

[66] United States v. Watson, 423 U.S. 411 (1976). *See also* United States v. Santana, 427 U.S. 38 (1976) (sustaining warrantless arrest of suspect in her home when she was initially approached in her doorway and then retreated into house). However, a suspect arrested on probable cause but without a warrant is entitled to a prompt, nonadversary hearing under procedures designed to provide a fair and reliable determination of probable cause in order to keep the arrestee in custody. Gerstein v. Pugh, 420 U.S. 103 (1975). A "prompt" hearing now means a hearing that is administratively convenient. *See* County of Riverside v. McLaughlin, 500 U.S. 44, 56 (1991) (authorizing "as a general matter" detention for up to 48 hours without a probable-cause hearing, after which time the burden shifts to the government to demonstrate extraordinary circumstances justifying further detention).

[67] Payton v. New York, 445 U.S. 573 (1980) (voiding state law authorizing police to enter private residence without a warrant to make an arrest); Steagald v. United States, 451 U.S. 204 (1981) (officers with arrest warrant for A entered B's home without search warrant and discovered incriminating evidence; violated Fourth Amendment in absence of warrant to search the home); Hayes v. Florida, 470 U.S. 811 (1985) (officers went to suspect's home and took him to police station for fingerprinting).

[68] United States v. Mendenhall, 446 U.S. 544, 554 (1980) ("a person has been 'seized' within the meaning of the Fourth Amendment only if, in view of all the circumstances surrounding the incident, a reasonable person would have believed that he was not free to leave"). *See also* Reid v. Georgia, 448 U.S. 438 (1980); United States v. Brignoni-Ponce, 422 U.S. 873, 878 (1975); Terry v. Ohio, 392 U.S. 1, 16–19 (1968); Kaupp v. Texas, 538 U.S. 626 (2003). Apprehension by the use of deadly force is a seizure subject to the Fourth Amendment's reasonableness requirement. *See, e.g.*, Tennessee v. Garner, 471 U.S. 1 (1985) (police officer's fatal shooting of a fleeing suspect); Brower v. County of Inyo, 489 U.S. 593 (1989) (police roadblock designed to end car chase with fatal crash); Scott v. Harris, 550 U.S. 372 (2007) (police officer's ramming fleeing motorist's car from behind in attempt to stop him); Plumhoff v. Rickard, 572 U.S. ___, No. 12–1117, slip op. (2014) (police use of 15 gunshots to end a police chase).

[69] The justification must be made to a neutral magistrate, not to the arrestee. There is no constitutional requirement that an officer inform an arrestee of the rea-

that involve only a brief detention short of arrest, although the nature of the detention will determine whether probable cause or some reasonable and articulable suspicion is necessary.[70]

The Fourth Amendment does not require an officer to consider whether to issue a citation rather than arresting (and placing in custody) a person who has committed a minor offense—even a minor traffic offense. In *Atwater v. City of Lago Vista*,[71] the Court, even while acknowledging that the case before it involved "gratuitous humiliations imposed by a police officer who was (at best) exercising extremely poor judgment," refused to require that "case-by-case determinations of government need" to place traffic offenders in custody be subjected to a reasonableness inquiry, "lest every discretionary judgment in the field be converted into an occasion for constitutional review." [72] Citing some state statutes that limit warrantless arrests for minor offenses, the Court contended that the matter is better left to statutory rule than to application of broad constitutional principle.[73] Thus, *Atwater* and *County of Riverside v. McLaughlin* [74] together mean that—as far as the Constitution is concerned—police officers have almost unbridled discretion to decide whether to issue a summons for a minor traffic offense or whether instead to place the offending motorist in jail, where she may be kept for up to 48 hours with little recourse. Even when an arrest

---

son for his arrest. Devenpeck v. Alford, 543 U.S. 146, 155 (2004) (the offense for which there is probable cause to arrest need not be closely related to the offense stated by the officer at the time of arrest).

[70] Delaware v. Prouse, 440 U.S. 648, 650 (1979) ("unreasonable seizure . . . to stop an automobile . . . for the purpose of checking the driving license of the operator and the registration of the car, where there is neither probable cause to believe nor reasonable suspicion" that a law was violated); Brown v. Texas, 443 U.S. 47, 51 (1979) (detaining a person for the purpose of requiring him to identify himself constitutes a seizure requiring a "reasonable, articulable suspicion that a crime had just been, was being, or was about to be committed"); Reid v. Georgia, 448 U.S. 438, 441 (1980) (requesting ticket stubs and identification from persons disembarking from plane not reasonable where stated justifications would apply to "a very large category of innocent travelers," *e.g.*, travelers arrived from "a principal place of origin of cocaine"); Michigan v. Summers, 452 U.S. 692, 705 (1981) ("it is constitutionally reasonable to require that [a] citizen . . . remain while officers of the law execute a valid warrant to search his home"); Illinois v. McArthur, 531 U.S. 326 (2001) (approving "securing" of premises, preventing homeowner from reentering, while a search warrant is obtained); Los Angeles County v. Rettele, 550 U.S. 609 (2007) (where deputies executing a search warrant did not know that the house being searched had recently been sold, it was reasonable to hold new homeowners, who had been sleeping in the nude, at gunpoint for one to two minutes without allowing them to dress or cover themselves, even though the deputies knew that the homeowners were of a different race from the suspects named in the warrant).

[71] 532 U.S. 318 (2001).

[72] 532 U.S. at 346–47.

[73] 532 U.S. at 352.

[74] 500 U.S. 44 (1991).

for a minor offense is prohibited by state law, the arrest will not violate the Fourth Amendment if it was based on probable cause.[75]

Until relatively recently, the legality of arrests was seldom litigated in the Supreme Court because of the rule that a person detained pursuant to an arbitrary seizure—unlike evidence obtained as a result of an unlawful search—remains subject to custody and presentation to court.[76] But the application of self-incrimination and other exclusionary rules to the states and the heightening of their scope in state and federal cases alike brought forth the rule that verbal evidence, confessions, and other admissions, like all derivative evidence obtained as a result of unlawful seizures, could be excluded.[77] Thus, a confession made by one illegally in custody must be suppressed, unless the causal connection between the illegal arrest and the confession had become so attenuated that the latter should not be deemed "tainted" by the former.[78] Similarly, fingerprints and other physical evidence obtained as a result of an unlawful arrest must be suppressed.[79]

---

[75] Virginia v. Moore, 128 S. Ct. 1598 (2008). *See also* Heien v. North Carolina, 574 U.S. ___, No. 13–604, slip op. at 5 (2014) (holding that a mistake of law can give rise to the reasonable suspicion necessary to uphold the seizure of a vehicle). The law enforcement officer in *Heien* had stopped the vehicle because it had only one working brake light, which the officer understood to be a violation of the North Carolina vehicle code. *Id.* at 2. However, a North Carolina court subsequently held, in a case of first impression, that the vehicle code only requires one working brake light. *Id.* at 3. In holding that reasonable suspicion can rest on a mistaken understanding of a legal prohibition, a majority of the Supreme Court noted prior cases finding that mistakes of fact do not preclude reasonable suspicion and concluded that "reasonable men make mistakes of law, too." *Id.* at 5–6 (citing Illinois v. Rodriguez, 497 U.S. 177, 183–86 (1990), and Hill v. California, 401 U.S. 797, 802–05 (1971), as cases involving mistakes of fact).

[76] Ker v. Illinois, 119 U.S. 436, 440 (1886); *see also* Albrecht v. United States, 273 U.S. 1 (1927); Frisbie v. Collins, 342 U.S. 519 (1952).

[77] Wong Sun v. United States, 371 U.S. 471 (1963). Such evidence is the "fruit of the poisonous tree," Nardone v. United States, 308 U.S. 338, 341 (1939), that is, evidence derived from the original illegality. Previously, if confessions were voluntary for purposes of the self-incrimination clause, they were admissible notwithstanding any prior official illegality. Colombe v. Connecticut, 367 U.S. 568 (1961).

[78] Although there is a presumption that the illegal arrest is the cause of the subsequent confession, the presumption is rebuttable by a showing that the confession is the result of "an intervening . . . act of free will." Wong Sun v. United States, 371 U.S. 471, 486 (1963). The factors used to determine whether the taint has been dissipated are the time between the illegal arrest and the confession, whether there were intervening circumstances (such as consultation with others, *Miranda* warnings, etc.), and the degree of flagrancy and purposefulness of the official conduct. Brown v. Illinois, 422 U.S. 590 (1975) (*Miranda* warnings alone insufficient); Dunaway v. New York, 442 U.S. 200 (1979); Taylor v. Alabama, 457 U.S. 687 (1982); Kaupp v. Texas, 538 U.S. 626 (2003). In Johnson v. Louisiana, 406 U.S. 356 (1972), the fact that the suspect had been taken before a magistrate who advised him of his rights and set bail, after which he confessed, established a sufficient intervening circumstance.

[79] Davis v. Mississippi, 394 U.S. 721 (1969); Taylor v. Alabama, 457 U.S. 687 (1982). In United States v. Crews, 445 U.S. 463 (1980), the Court, unanimously but

Searches and Inspections in Noncriminal Cases.—Certain early cases held that the Fourth Amendment was applicable only when a search was undertaken for criminal investigatory purposes,[80] and the Supreme Court until recently employed a reasonableness test for such searches without requiring either a warrant or probable cause in the absence of a warrant.[81] But, in 1967, the Court in two cases held that administrative inspections to detect building code violations must be undertaken pursuant to warrant if the occupant objects.[82] "We may agree that a routine inspection of the physical condition of private property is a less hostile intrusion than the typical policeman's search for the fruits and instrumentalities of crime. . . . But we cannot agree that the Fourth Amendment interests at stake in these inspection cases are merely 'peripheral.' It is surely anomalous to say that the individual and his private property are fully protected by the Fourth Amendment only when the individual is suspected of criminal behavior."[83] Certain administrative inspections used to enforce regulatory schemes with regard to such items as alcohol and firearms are, however, exempt from the Fourth Amendment warrant requirement and may be authorized simply by statute.[84]

Camara and *See* were reaffirmed in *Marshall v. Barlow's, Inc.*,[85] in which the Court held to violate the Fourth Amendment a provision of the Occupational Safety and Health Act that authorized federal inspectors to search the work area of any employment facility covered by the Act for safety hazards and violations of regulations,

---

for a variety of reasons, held proper the identification in court of a defendant, who had been wrongly arrested without probable cause, by the crime victim. The court identification was not tainted by either the arrest or the subsequent in-custody identification. *See also* Hayes v. Florida, 470 U.S. 811, 815 (1985), suggesting in dictum that a "narrowly circumscribed procedure for fingerprinting detentions on less than probable cause" may be permissible.

[80] *In re* Strouse, 23 Fed. Cas. 261 (No. 13,548) (D. Nev. 1871); *In re* Meador, 16 Fed. Cas. 1294, 1299 (No. 9375) (N.D. Ga. 1869).

[81] Abel v. United States, 362 U.S. 217 (1960); Frank v. Maryland, 359 U.S. 360 (1959); Oklahoma Press Pub. Co. v. Walling, 327 U.S. 186 (1946).

[82] Camara v. Municipal Court, 387 U.S. 523 (1967) (home); See v. City of Seattle, 387 U.S. 541 (1967) (commercial warehouse).

[83] Camara v. Municipal Court, 387 U.S. 523, 530 (1967).

[84] Colonnade Catering Corp. v. United States, 397 U.S. 72 (1970); United States v. Biswell, 406 U.S. 311 (1972). *Colonnade*, involving liquor, was based on the long history of close supervision of the industry. *Biswell*, involving firearms, introduced factors that were subsequently to prove significant. Thus, although the statute was of recent enactment, firearms constituted a pervasively regulated industry, so that dealers had no reasonable expectation of privacy, because the law provides for regular inspections. Further, warrantless inspections were needed for effective enforcement of the statute.

[85] 436 U.S. 307 (1978). Dissenting, Justice Stevens, with Justices Rehnquist and Blackmun, argued that not the warrant clause but the reasonableness clause should govern administrative inspections. Id. at 325.

without a warrant or other legal process. The liquor and firearms exceptions were distinguished on the basis that those industries had a long tradition of close government supervision, so that a person in those businesses gave up his privacy expectations. But OSHA was a relatively recent statute and it regulated practically every business in or affecting interstate commerce; it was not open to a legislature to extend regulation and then follow it with warrantless inspections. Additionally, OSHA inspectors had unbounded discretion in choosing which businesses to inspect and when to do so, leaving businesses at the mercy of possibly arbitrary actions and certainly with no assurances as to limitation on scope and standards of inspections. Further, warrantless inspections were not necessary to serve an important governmental interest, as most businesses would consent to inspection and it was not inconvenient to require OSHA to resort to an administrative warrant in order to inspect sites where consent was refused.[86]

In *Donovan v. Dewey*,[87] however, the Court seemingly limited *Barlow's* reach and articulated a new standard that appeared to permit extensive governmental inspection of commercial property without a warrant. Under the Federal Mine Safety and Health Act, governing underground and surface mines (including stone quarries), federal officers are directed to inspect underground mines at least four times a year and surface mines at least twice a year, pursuant to extensive regulations as to standards of safety. The statute specifically provides for absence of advanced notice and requires the Secretary of Labor to institute court actions for injunctive and other relief in cases in which inspectors are denied admission. Sustaining the statute, the Court proclaimed that government had a "greater latitude" to conduct warrantless inspections of commercial prop-

---

[86] Administrative warrants issued on the basis of less than probable cause but only on a showing that a specific business had been chosen for inspection on the basis of a general administrative plan would suffice. Even without a necessity for probable cause, the requirement would assure the interposition of a neutral officer to establish that the inspection was reasonable and was properly authorized. 436 U.S. at 321, 323. The dissenters objected that the warrant clause was being constitutionally diluted. Id. at 325. Administrative warrants were approved also in Camara v. Municipal Court, 387 U.S. 523, 538 (1967). Previously, one of the reasons given for finding administrative and noncriminal inspections not covered by the Fourth Amendment was the fact that the warrant clause would be as rigorously applied to them as to criminal searches and seizures. Frank v. Maryland, 359 U.S. 360, 373 (1959). *See also* Almeida-Sanchez v. United States, 413 U.S. 266, 275 (1973) (Justice Powell concurring) (suggesting a similar administrative warrant procedure empowering police and immigration officers to conduct roving searches of automobiles in areas near the Nation's borders); id. at 270 n.3 (indicating that majority Justices were divided on the validity of such area search warrants); id. at 288 (dissenting Justice White indicating approval); United States v. Martinez-Fuerte, 428 U.S. 543, 547 n.2, 562 n.15 (1976).

[87] 452 U.S. 594 (1981).

erty than of homes, because of "the fact that the expectation of privacy that the owner of commercial property enjoys in such property differs significantly from the sanctity accorded an individual's home, and that this privacy interest may, in certain circumstances, be adequately protected by regulatory schemes authorizing warrantless inspections."[88]

Dewey was distinguished from *Barlow's* in several ways. First, *Dewey* involved a single industry, unlike the broad coverage in *Barlow's*. Second, the OSHA statute gave minimal direction to inspectors as to time, scope, and frequency of inspections, while FMSHA specified a regular number of inspections pursuant to standards. Third, deference was due Congress's determination that unannounced inspections were necessary if the safety laws were to be effectively enforced. Fourth, FMSHA provided businesses the opportunity to contest the search by resisting in the civil proceeding the Secretary had to bring if consent was denied.[89] The standard of a long tradition of government supervision permitting warrantless inspections was dispensed with, because it would lead to "absurd results," in that new and emerging industries posing great hazards would escape regulation.[90]

Dewey was applied in *New York v. Burger*[91] to inspection of automobile junkyards and vehicle dismantling operations, a situation where there is considerable overlap between administrative and penal objectives. Applying the *Dewey* three-part test, the Court concluded that New York has a substantial interest in stemming the tide of automobile thefts, that regulation of vehicle dismantling reasonably serves that interest, and that statutory safeguards provided adequate substitute for a warrant requirement. The Court rejected the suggestion that the warrantless inspection provisions were designed as an expedient means of enforcing the penal laws, and instead saw narrower, valid regulatory purposes to be served, such as establishing a system for tracking stolen automobiles and parts, and enhancing the ability of legitimate businesses to compete. "[A] State can address a major social problem *both* by way of an admin-

[88] Donovan v. Dewey, 452 U.S. 594, 598–99 (1981).

[89] 452 U.S. at 596–97, 604–05. Pursuant to the statute, however, the Secretary has promulgated regulations providing for the assessment of civil penalties for denial of entry and Dewey had been assessed a penalty of $1,000. Id. at 597 n.3. It was also true in *Barlow's* that the government resorted to civil process upon refusal to admit. 436 U.S. at 317 & n.12.

[90] Donovan v. Dewey, 452 U.S. 594, 606 (1981). Duration of regulation will now be a factor in assessing the legitimate expectation of privacy of a business. Id. *Accord*, New York v. Burger, 482 U.S. 691 (1987) (although duration of regulation of vehicle dismantling was relatively brief, history of regulation of junk business generally was lengthy, and current regulation of dismantling was extensive).

[91] 482 U.S. 691 (1987).

istrative scheme *and* through penal sanctions," the Court declared; in such circumstances warrantless administrative searches are permissible in spite of the fact that evidence of criminal activity may well be uncovered in the process.[92]

Most recently, however, in *City of Los Angeles v. Patel*, the Court declined to extend the "more relaxed standard" applicable to searches of closely regulated businesses to hotels when invalidating a Los Angeles ordinance that gave police the ability to inspect hotel registration records without advance notice and carried a six-month term of imprisonment and a $1,000 fine for hotel operators who failed to make such records available.[93] The *Patel* Court, characterizing inspections pursuant to this ordinance as "administrative searches,"[94] held "that a hotel owner must be afforded an *opportunity* to have a neutral decision maker review an officer's demand to search the registry before he or she faces penalties for failing to comply" for such a search to be permissible under the Fourth Amendment.[95] In so doing, the Court expressly declined to treat the hotel industry as a "closely regulated" industry subject to the more relaxed standard applied in *Dewey* and *Burger* on the grounds that doing so would "permit what has always been a narrow exception to swallow the rule."[96] The Court emphasized that, over the prior 45 years, it had recognized only four industries as having "such a history of government oversight that no reasonable expectation of privacy . . . could exist for a proprietor over the stock of such an enterprise."[97] These four industries involve liquor sales, firearms dealing, mining, and running an automobile junkyard, and the Court distinguished hotel operations from these industries, in part, because "nothing inherent in the operation of hotels poses a clear and significant risk

---

[92] 482 U.S. at 712 (emphasis in original).

[93] 576 U.S. ___, No. 13–1175, slip op. at 14 (2014). *Patel* involved a facial, rather than an as-applied, challenge to the Los Angeles ordinance. The Court clarified that facial challenges under the Fourth Amendment are "not categorically barred or especially disfavored." *Id.* at 4. Some had apparently taken the Court's earlier statement in *Sibron v. New York*, 392 U.S. 40 (1968), that "[t]he constitutional validity of a warrantless search is pre-eminently the sort of question which can only be decided in the concrete factual context of the individual case," *id.* at 59, to foreclose facial Fourth Amendment challenges. *Patel*, slip op. at 5. However, the *Patel* Court construed *Sibron*'s language to mean only that "claims for facial relief under the Fourth Amendment are unlikely to succeed when there is substantial ambiguity as to what conduct a statute authorizes." *Id.*

[94] *Patel*, slip op. at 10.

[95] *Id.* at 11. The Court further noted that actual pre-compliance review need only occur in those "rare instances" where a hotel owner objects to turning over the registry, and that the Court has never "attempted to prescribe" the exact form of such review. *Id.* at 10–11.

[96] *Id.* at 14.

[97] *Id.* (quoting *Barlow's*, 436 U.S. at 313).

to the public welfare." [98] However, the Court also suggested that, even if hotels were to be seen as pervasively regulated, the Los Angeles ordinance would still be deemed unreasonable because (1) there was no substantial government interest informing the regulatory scheme; (2) warrantless inspections were not necessary to further the government's purpose; and (3) the inspection program did not provide, in terms of the certainty and regularity of its application, a constitutionally adequate substitute for a warrant. [99]

In other contexts, not directly concerned with whether an industry is comprehensively regulated, the Court has also elaborated the constitutional requirements affecting administrative inspections and searches. In *Michigan v. Tyler*, [100] for example, it subdivided the process by which an investigation of the cause of a fire may be conducted. Entry to fight the fire is, of course, an exception based on exigent circumstances, and no warrant or consent is needed; fire fighters on the scene may seize evidence relating to the cause under the plain view doctrine. Additional entries to investigate the cause of the fire must be made pursuant to warrant procedures governing administrative searches. Evidence of arson discovered in the course of such an administrative inspection is admissible at trial, but if the investigator finds probable cause to believe that arson has occurred and requires further access to gather evidence for a possible prosecution, he must obtain a criminal search warrant. [101]

One curious case has approved a system of "home visits" by welfare caseworkers, in which the recipients are required to admit the worker or lose eligibility for benefits. [102] In another unusual case, the Court held that a sheriff's assistance to a trailer park owner in

---

[98] *Id.* The majority further stated that the existence of regulations requiring hotels to maintain licenses, collect taxes, and take other actions did not establish a "comprehensive scheme of regulation" distinguishing hotels from other industries. *Id.* at 15. It also opined that the historical practice of treating hotels as public accommodations does not necessarily mean that hotels are to be treated as comprehensively regulated for purposes of warrantless searches. *Id.* at 14–15.

[99] *Id.* at 16. Specifically, the Court noted that the government's alleged interest in ensuring that hotel operators not falsify their records, as they could if given an opportunity for pre-compliance review, applied to every recordkeeping requirement. *Id.* The Court similarly noted that there were other ways to further the city's interest in warrantless inspections (e.g., *ex parte* warrants) and that the ordinance failed to sufficiently constrain a police officer's discretion as to which hotels to search and under what circumstances. *Id.*

[100] 436 U.S. 499 (1978).

[101] The Court also held that, after the fire was extinguished, if fire investigators were unable to proceed at the moment, because of dark, steam, and smoke, it was proper for them to leave and return at daylight without any necessity of complying with its mandate for administrative or criminal warrants. 436 U.S. at 510–11. *But cf.* Michigan v. Clifford, 464 U.S. 287 (1984) (no such justification for search of private residence begun at 1:30 p.m. when fire had been extinguished at 7 a.m.).

[102] Wyman v. James, 400 U.S. 309 (1971). It is not clear what rationale the majority used. It appears to have proceeded on the assumption that a "home visit" was

disconnecting and removing a mobile home constituted a "seizure" of the home.[103]

In addition, there are now a number of situations, some of them analogous to administrative searches, where "'special needs' beyond normal law enforcement . . . justify departures from the usual warrant and probable cause requirements."[104] In one of these cases the Court, without acknowledging the magnitude of the leap from one context to another, has taken the *Dewey/Burger* rationale—developed to justify warrantless searches of business establishments—and applied it to justify the significant intrusion into personal privacy represented by urinalysis drug testing. Because of the history of pervasive regulation of the railroad industry, the Court reasoned, railroad employees have a diminished expectation of privacy that makes mandatory urinalysis less intrusive and more reasonable.[105]

With respect to automobiles, the holdings are mixed. Random stops of automobiles to check drivers' licenses, vehicle registrations, and safety conditions were condemned as too intrusive; the degree to which random stops would advance the legitimate governmental interests involved did not outweigh the individual's legitimate expectations of privacy.[106] On the other hand, in *South Da-*

---

not a search and that the Fourth Amendment does not apply when criminal prosecution is not threatened. Neither premise is valid under *Camara* and its progeny, although *Camara* preceded *Wyman.* Presumably, the case would today be analyzed under the expectation of privacy/need/structural protection theory of the more recent cases.

[103] Soldal v. Cook County, 506 U.S. 56, 61 (1992) (home "was not only seized, it literally was carried away, giving new meaning to the term 'mobile home'").

[104] City of Ontario v. Quon, 560 U.S. ___, No. 08–1332, slip op. (2010) (reasonableness test for obtaining and reviewing transcripts of on-duty text messages of police officer using government-issued equipment); Griffin v. Wisconsin, 483 U.S. 868, 873 (1987) (administrative needs of probation system justify warrantless searches of probationers' homes on less than probable cause); Hudson v. Palmer, 468 U.S. 517, 526 (1984) (no Fourth Amendment protection from search of prison cell); New Jersey v. T.L.O., 469 U.S. 325 (1985) (simple reasonableness standard governs searches of students' persons and effects by public school authorities); O'Connor v. Ortega, 480 U.S. 709 (1987) (reasonableness test for work-related searches of employees' offices by government employer); Skinner v. Railway Labor Executives' Ass'n, 489 U.S. 602 (1989) (neither probable cause nor individualized suspicion is necessary for mandatory drug testing of railway employees involved in accidents or safety violations). All of these cases are discussed *infra* under the general heading "Valid Searches and Seizures Without Warrants."

[105] *Skinner,* 489 U.S. at 627.

[106] Delaware v. Prouse, 440 U.S. 648 (1979). Standards applied in this case had been developed in the contexts of automobile stops at fixed points or by roving patrols in border situations. Almeida-Sanchez v. United States, 413 U.S. 266 (1973); United States v. Brignoni-Ponce, 422 U.S. 873 (1975); United States v. Ortiz, 422 U.S. 891 (1975); United States v. Martinez-Fuerte, 428 U.S. 543 (1976).

kota v. Opperman,[107] the Court sustained the admission of evidence found when police impounded an automobile from a public street for multiple parking violations and entered the car to secure and inventory valuables for safekeeping. Marijuana was discovered in the glove compartment.

Searches and Seizures Pursuant to Warrant

Emphasis upon the necessity of warrants places the judgment of an independent magistrate between law enforcement officers and the privacy of citizens, authorizes invasion of that privacy only upon a showing that constitutes probable cause, and limits that invasion by specification of the person to be seized, the place to be searched, and the evidence to be sought.[108] Although a warrant is issued *ex parte*, its validity may be contested in a subsequent suppression hearing if incriminating evidence is found and a prosecution is brought.[109]

Issuance by Neutral Magistrate.—In numerous cases, the Court has referred to the necessity that warrants be issued by a "judicial officer" or a "magistrate."[110] "The point of the Fourth Amendment, which often is not grasped by zealous officers, is not that it denies law enforcement the support of the usual inferences which reasonable men draw from evidence. Its protection consists in requiring that those inferences be drawn by a neutral and detached magistrate instead of being judged by the officer engaged in the often competitive enterprise of ferreting out crime. Any assumption that evi-

---

[107] 428 U.S. 364 (1976). *See also* Cady v. Dombrowski, 413 U.S. 433 (1973) (sustaining admission of criminal evidence found when police conducted a warrantless search of an out-of-state policeman's automobile following an accident, in order to find and safeguard his service revolver). The Court in both cases emphasized the reduced expectation of privacy in automobiles and the noncriminal purposes of the searches.

[108] Although the exceptions may be different for arrest warrants and search warrants, the requirements for the issuance of the two are the same. Aguilar v. Texas, 378 U.S. 108, 112 n.3 (1964). Also, the standards by which the validity of warrants are to be judged are the same, whether federal or state officers are involved. Ker v. California, 374 U.S. 23 (1963).

[109] Most often, in the suppression hearings, the defendant will challenge the sufficiency of the evidence presented to the magistrate to constitute probable cause. Spinelli v. United States, 393 U.S. 410 (1969); United States v. Harris, 403 U.S. 573 (1971). He may challenge the veracity of the statements used by the police to procure the warrant and otherwise contest the accuracy of the allegations going to establish probable cause, but the Court has carefully hedged his ability to do so. Franks v. Delaware, 438 U.S. 154 (1978). He may also question the power of the official issuing the warrant, Coolidge v. New Hampshire, 403 U.S. 443, 449–53 (1971), or the specificity of the particularity required. Marron v. United States, 275 U.S. 192 (1927).

[110] United States v. Lefkowitz, 285 U.S. 452, 464 (1932); Giordenello v. United States, 357 U.S. 480, 486 (1958); Jones v. United States, 362 U.S. 257, 270 (1960); Katz v. United States, 389 U.S. 347, 356 (1967); United States v. United States District Court, 407 U.S. 297, 321 (1972); United States v. Chadwick, 433 U.S. 1, 9 (1977); Lo-Ji Sales v. New York, 442 U.S. 319 (1979).

dence sufficient to support a magistrate's disinterested determination to issue a search warrant will justify the officers in making a search without a warrant would reduce the Amendment to a nullity and leave the people's homes secure only in the discretion of police officers." [111] These cases do not mean that only a judge or an official who is a lawyer may issue warrants, but they do stand for two tests of the validity of the power of the issuing party to so act. "He must be neutral and detached, and he must be capable of determining whether probable cause exists for the requested arrest or search." [112] The first test cannot be met when the issuing party is himself engaged in law enforcement activities,[113] but the Court has not required that an issuing party have that independence of tenure and guarantee of salary that characterizes federal judges.[114] And, in passing on the second test, the Court has been essentially pragmatic in assessing whether the issuing party possesses the capacity to determine probable cause.[115]

Probable Cause.—The concept of "probable cause" is central to the meaning of the warrant clause. Neither the Fourth Amendment nor the federal statutory provisions relevant to the area define "probable cause"; the definition is entirely a judicial construct. An applicant for a warrant must present to the magistrate facts sufficient to enable the officer himself to make a determination of probable cause. "In determining what is probable cause . . . [w]e are concerned only with the question whether the affiant had reasonable grounds at the time of his affidavit . . . for the belief that

---

[111] Johnson v. United States, 333 U.S. 10, 13–14 (1948).

[112] Shadwick v. City of Tampa, 407 U.S. 345, 354 (1972).

[113] Coolidge v. New Hampshire, 403 U.S. 443, 449–51 (1971) (warrant issued by state attorney general who was leading investigation and who as a justice of the peace was authorized to issue warrants); Mancusi v. DeForte, 392 U.S. 364, 370–72 (1968) (subpoena issued by district attorney could not qualify as a valid search warrant); Lo-Ji Sales v. New York, 442 U.S. 319 (1979) (justice of the peace issued open-ended search warrant for obscene materials, accompanied police during its execution, and made probable cause determinations at the scene as to particular items).

[114] Jones v. United States, 362 U.S. 257, 270–71 (1960) (approving issuance of warrants by United States Commissioners, many of whom were not lawyers and none of whom had any guarantees of tenure and salary); Shadwick v. City of Tampa, 407 U.S. 345 (1972) (approving issuance of arrest warrants for violation of city ordinances by city clerks who were assigned to and supervised by municipal court judges). The Court reserved the question "whether a State may lodge warrant authority in someone entirely outside the sphere of the judicial branch. Many persons may not qualify as the kind of 'public civil officers' we have come to associate with the term 'magistrate.' Had the Tampa clerk been entirely divorced from a judicial position, this case would have presented different considerations." Id. at 352.

[115] 407 U.S. at 350–54 (placing on defendant the burden of demonstrating that the issuing official lacks capacity to determine probable cause). *See also* Connally v. Georgia, 429 U.S. 245 (1977) (unsalaried justice of the peace who receives a sum of money for each warrant issued but nothing for reviewing and denying a warrant is not sufficiently detached).

the law was being violated on the premises to be searched; and if the apparent facts set out in the affidavit are such that a reasonably discreet and prudent man would be led to believe that there was a commission of the offense charged, there is probable cause justifying the issuance of a warrant." [116] Probable cause is to be determined according to "the factual and practical considerations of everyday life on which reasonable and prudent men, not legal technicians, act." [117] Warrants are favored in the law and their use will not be thwarted by a hypertechnical reading of the supporting affidavit and supporting testimony. [118] For the same reason, reviewing courts will accept evidence of a less "judicially competent or persuasive character than would have justified an officer in acting on his own without a warrant." [119] Courts will sustain the determination of probable cause so long as "there was substantial basis for [the magistrate] to conclude that" there was probable cause. [120]

Much litigation has concerned the sufficiency of the complaint to establish probable cause. Mere conclusory assertions are not enough. [121] In *United States v. Ventresca*, [122] however, an affidavit by a law enforcement officer asserting his belief that an illegal distill-

---

[116] Dumbra v. United States, 268 U.S. 435, 439, 441 (1925). "[T]he term 'probable cause' . . . means less than evidence which would justify condemnation." Lock v. United States, 11 U.S. (7 Cr.) 339, 348 (1813). *See* Steele v. United States, 267 U.S. 498, 504–05 (1925). It may rest upon evidence that is not legally competent in a criminal trial, Draper v. United States, 358 U.S. 307, 311 (1959), and it need not be sufficient to prove guilt in a criminal trial. Brinegar v. United States, 338 U.S. 160, 173 (1949). *See* United States v. Ventresca, 380 U.S. 102, 107–08 (1965). An "anticipatory" warrant does not violate the Fourth Amendment as long as there is probable cause to believe that the condition precedent to execution of the search warrant will occur and that, once it has occurred, "there is a fair probability that contraband or evidence of a crime will be found in a specified place." United States v. Grubbs, 547 U.S. 90, 95 (2006), quoting Illinois v. Gates, 462 U.S. 213, 238 (1983). "An anticipatory warrant is 'a warrant based upon an affidavit showing probable cause that at some future time (but not presently) certain evidence of a crime will be located at a specified place.'" 547 U.S. at 94.

[117] Brinegar v. United States, 338 U.S. 160, 175 (1949).

[118] United States v. Ventresca, 380 U.S. 102, 108–09 (1965).

[119] Jones v. United States, 362 U.S. 257, 270–71 (1960). Similarly, the preference for proceeding by warrant leads to a stricter rule for appellate review of trial court decisions on warrantless stops and searches than is employed to review probable cause to issue a warrant. Ornelas v. United States, 517 U.S. 690 (1996) (determinations of reasonable suspicion to stop and probable cause to search without a warrant should be subjected to *de novo* appellate review).

[120] Aguilar v. Texas, 378 U.S. 108, 111 (1964). It must be emphasized that the issuing party "must judge for himself the persuasiveness of the facts relied on by a [complainant] to show probable cause." Giordenello v. United States, 357 U.S. 480, 486 (1958). An insufficient affidavit cannot be rehabilitated by testimony after issuance concerning information possessed by the affiant but not disclosed to the magistrate. Whiteley v. Warden, 401 U.S. 560 (1971).

[121] Byars v. United States, 273 U.S. 28 (1927) (affiant stated he "has good reason to believe and does believe" that defendant has contraband materials in his possession); Giordenello v. United States, 357 U.S. 480 (1958) (complainant merely stated

ery was being operated in a certain place, explaining that the belief was based upon his own observations and upon those of fellow investigators, and detailing a substantial amount of these personal observations clearly supporting the stated belief, was held to be sufficient to constitute probable cause. "Recital of some of the underlying circumstances in the affidavit is essential," the Court said, observing that "where these circumstances are detailed, where reason for crediting the source of the information is given, and when a magistrate has found probable cause," the reliance on the warrant process should not be deterred by insistence on too stringent a showing.[123]

Requirements for establishing probable cause through reliance on information received from an informant has divided the Court in several cases. Although involving a warrantless arrest, *Draper v. United States* [124] may be said to have begun the line of cases. A previously reliable, named informant reported to an officer that the defendant would arrive with narcotics on a particular train, and described the clothes he would be wearing and the bag he would be carrying; the informant, however, gave no basis for his information. FBI agents met the train, observed that the defendant fully fit the description, and arrested him. The Court held that the corroboration of part of the informer's tip established probable cause to support the arrest. A case involving a search warrant, *Jones v. United States*,[125] apparently considered the affidavit as a whole to see whether the tip plus the corroborating information provided a substantial basis for finding probable cause, but the affidavit also set forth the reliability of the informer and sufficient detail to indicate that the tip was based on the informant's personal observation. *Aguilar v. Texas* [126] held insufficient an affidavit that merely asserted that the police had "reliable information from a credible person" that narcotics were in a certain place, and held that when the affiant relies on an informant's tip he must present two types of evidence to the magistrate. First, the affidavit must indicate the informant's basis of knowledge—the circumstances from which the

his conclusion that defendant had committed a crime). *See also* Nathanson v. United States, 290 U.S. 41 (1933).

[122] 380 U.S. 102 (1965).

[123] 380 U.S. at 109.

[124] 358 U.S. 307 (1959). For another case applying essentially the same probable cause standard to warrantless arrests as govern arrests by warrant, *see* McCray v. Illinois, 386 U.S. 300 (1967) (informant's statement to arresting officers met *Aguilar* probable cause standard). *See also* Whitely v. Warden, 401 U.S. 560, 566 (1971) (standards must be "at least as stringent" for warrantless arrest as for obtaining warrant).

[125] 362 U.S. 257 (1960).

[126] 378 U.S. 108 (1964).

informant concluded that evidence was present or that crimes had been committed—and, second, the affiant must present information that would permit the magistrate to decide whether or not the informant was trustworthy. Then, in *Spinelli v. United States*,[127] the Court applied *Aguilar* in a situation in which the affidavit contained both an informant's tip and police information of a corroborating nature.

The Court rejected the "totality" test derived from *Jones* and held that the informant's tip and the corroborating evidence must be separately considered. The tip was rejected because the affidavit contained neither any information which showed the basis of the tip nor any information which showed the informant's credibility. The corroborating evidence was rejected as insufficient because it did not establish any element of criminality but merely related to details which were innocent in themselves. No additional corroborating weight was due as a result of the bald police assertion that defendant was a known gambler, although the tip related to gambling. Returning to the totality test, however, the Court in *United States v. Harris*[128] approved a warrant issued largely on an informer's tip that over a two-year period he had purchased illegal whiskey from the defendant at the defendant's residence, most recently within two weeks of the tip. The affidavit contained rather detailed information about the concealment of the whiskey, and asserted that the informer was a "prudent person," that defendant had a reputation as a bootlegger, that other persons had supplied similar information about him, and that he had been found in control of illegal whiskey within the previous four years. The Court determined that the detailed nature of the tip, the personal observation thus revealed, and the fact that the informer had admitted to criminal behavior by his purchase of whiskey were sufficient to enable the magistrate to find him reliable, and that the supporting evidence, including defendant's reputation, could supplement this determination.

The Court expressly abandoned the two-part *Aguilar-Spinelli* test and returned to the "totality of the circumstances" approach to evaluate probable cause based on an informant's tip in *Illinois v. Gates*.[129] The main defect of the two-part test, Justice Rehnquist concluded

---

[127] 393 U.S. 410 (1969). Both concurring and dissenting Justices recognized tension between *Draper* and *Aguilar*. *See* id. at 423 (Justice White concurring), id. at 429 (Justice Black dissenting and advocating the overruling of *Aguilar*).

[128] 403 U.S. 573 (1971). *See also* Adams v. Williams, 407 U.S. 143, 147 (1972) (approving warrantless stop of motorist based on informant's tip that "may have been insufficient" under *Aguilar* and *Spinelli* as basis for warrant).

[129] 462 U.S. 213 (1983). Justice Rehnquist's opinion of the Court was joined by Chief Justice Burger and by Justices Blackmun, Powell, and O'Connor. Justices Brennan, Marshall, and Stevens dissented.

for the Court, was in treating an informant's reliability and his basis for knowledge as independent requirements. Instead, "a deficiency in one may be compensated for, in determining the overall reliability of a tip, by a strong showing as to the other, or by some other indicia of reliability."[130] In evaluating probable cause, "[t]he task of the issuing magistrate is simply to make a practical, commonsense decision whether, given all the circumstances set forth in the affidavit before him, including the 'veracity' and 'basis of knowledge' of persons supplying hearsay information, there is a fair probability that contraband or evidence of a crime will be found in a particular place."[131]

Particularity.—"The requirement that warrants shall particularly describe the things to be seized makes general searches under them impossible and prevents the seizure of one thing under a warrant describing another. As to what is to be taken, nothing is left to the discretion of the officer executing the warrant."[132] This requirement thus acts to limit the scope of the search, as the executing officers should be limited to looking in places where the described object could be expected to be found.[133] The purpose of the particularity requirement extends beyond prevention of general searches; it also assures the person whose property is being searched of the lawful authority of the executing officer and of the limits of his power to search. It follows, therefore, that the warrant itself must describe with particularity the items to be seized, or that such itemization must appear in documents incorporated by reference in

---

[130] 462 U.S. at 213.

[131] 462 U.S. at 238. For an application of the *Gates* "totality of the circumstances" test to the warrantless search of a vehicle by a police officer, see, e.g. *Florida v. Harris*, 568 U.S. ___, No. 11–817, slip op. (2013).

[132] Marron v. United States, 275 U.S. 192, 196 (1927). *See* Stanford v. Texas, 379 U.S. 476 (1965). Of course, police who are lawfully on the premises pursuant to a warrant may seize evidence of crime in "plain view" even if that evidence is not described in the warrant. Coolidge v. New Hampshire, 403 U.S. 443, 464–71 (1971).

[133] In Terry v. Ohio, 392 U.S. 1, 17–19, (1968), the Court wrote: "This Court has held in the past that a search which is reasonable at its inception may violate the Fourth Amendment by virtue of its intolerable intensity and scope. Kremen v. United States, 353 U.S. 346 (1957); Go-Bart Importing Co. v. United States, 282 U.S. 344, 356–58 (1931); see United States v. Di Re, 332 U.S. 581, 586–87 (1948). The scope of the search must be 'strictly tied to and justified by' the circumstances which rendered its initiation permissible. Warden v. Hayden, 387 U.S. 294, 310 (1967) (Justice Fortas concurring); see, *e.g.*, Preston v. United States, 376 U.S. 364, 367–368 (1964); Agnello v. United States, 296 U.S. 20, 30–31 (1925)." *See also* Andresen v. Maryland, 427 U.S. 463, 470–82 (1976), and id. at 484, 492–93 (Justice Brennan dissenting). In Stanley v. Georgia, 394 U.S. 557, 569 (1969), Justices Stewart, Brennan, and White would have based the decision on the principle that a valid warrant for gambling paraphernalia did not authorize police upon discovering motion picture films in the course of the search to project the films to learn their contents.

the warrant and actually shown to the person whose property is to be searched.[134]

First Amendment Bearing on Probable Cause and Particularity.—Where the warrant process is used to authorize seizure of books and other items that may be protected by the First Amendment, the Court has required government to observe more exacting standards than in other cases.[135] Seizure of materials arguably protected by the First Amendment is a form of prior restraint that requires strict observance of the Fourth Amendment. At a minimum, a warrant is required, and additional safeguards may be required for large-scale seizures. Thus, in *Marcus v. Search Warrant*,[136] the seizure of 11,000 copies of 280 publications pursuant to warrant issued *ex parte* by a magistrate who had not examined any of the publications but who had relied on the conclusory affidavit of a policeman was voided. Failure to scrutinize the materials and to particularize the items to be seized was deemed inadequate, and it was further noted that police "were provided with no guide to the exercise of informed discretion, because there was no step in the procedure before seizure designed to focus searchingly on the question of obscenity."[137] A state procedure that was designed to comply with *Marcus* by the presentation of copies of books to be seized to the magistrate for his scrutiny prior to issuance of a warrant was nonetheless found inadequate by a plurality of the Court, which concluded that "since the warrant here authorized the sheriff to seize all copies of the specified titles, and since [appellant] was not afforded a hearing on the question of the obscenity even of the seven novels [seven of 59 listed titles were reviewed by the magistrate] before the warrant issued, the procedure was . . . constitutionally deficient."[138]

Confusion remains, however, about the necessity for and the character of prior adversary hearings on the issue of obscenity. In a later decision the Court held that, with adequate safeguards, no pre-

---

[134] Groh v. Ramirez, 540 U.S. 551 (2004) (a search based on a warrant that did not describe the items to be seized was "plainly invalid"; particularity contained in supporting documents not cross-referenced by the warrant and not accompanying the warrant is insufficient); United States v. Grubbs, 547 U.S. 90, 97, 99 (2006) (because the language of the Fourth Amendment "specifies only two matters that must be 'particularly describ[ed]' in the warrant: 'the place to be searched' and 'the persons or things to be seized[,]' . . . the Fourth Amendment does not require that the triggering condition for an anticipatory warrant be set forth in the warrant itself."

[135] Marcus v. Search Warrant, 367 U.S. 717, 730–31 (1961); Stanford v. Texas, 379 U.S. 476, 485 (1965). For First Amendment implications of seizures under the Federal Racketeer Influenced and Corrupt Organizations Act (RICO), see First Amendment: Obscenity and Prior Restraint.

[136] 367 U.S. 717 (1961). *See* Kingsley Books v. Brown, 354 U.S. 436 (1957).

[137] Marcus v. Search Warrant, 367 U.S. 717, 732 (1961).

[138] A Quantity of Books v. Kansas, 378 U.S. 205, 210 (1964).

seizure adversary hearing on the issue of obscenity is required if the film is seized not for the purpose of destruction as contraband (the purpose in *Marcus* and *A Quantity of Books*), but instead to preserve a copy for evidence.[139] It is constitutionally permissible to seize a copy of a film pursuant to a warrant as long as there is a prompt post-seizure adversary hearing on the obscenity issue. Until there is a judicial determination of obscenity, the Court advised, the film may continue to be exhibited; if no other copy is available either a copy of it must be made from the seized film or the film itself must be returned.[140]

The seizure of a film without the authority of a constitutionally sufficient warrant is invalid; seizure cannot be justified as incidental to arrest, as the determination of obscenity may not be made by the officer himself.[141] Nor may a warrant issue based "solely on the conclusory assertions of the police officer without any inquiry by the [magistrate] into the factual basis for the officer's conclusions."[142] Instead, a warrant must be "supported by affidavits setting forth specific facts in order that the issuing magistrate may 'focus searchingly on the question of obscenity.'"[143] This does not mean, however, that a higher standard of probable cause is required in order to obtain a warrant to seize materials protected by the First Amendment. "Our reference in *Roaden* to a 'higher hurdle . . . of reasonableness' was not intended to establish a 'higher' standard of probable cause for the issuance of a warrant to seize books or films, but instead related to the more basic requirement, imposed by that decision, that the police not rely on the 'exigency' exception to the Fourth Amendment warrant requirement, but instead obtain a warrant from a magistrate . . . .'"[144]

In *Stanford v. Texas*,[145] the Court voided a seizure of more than 2,000 books, pamphlets, and other documents pursuant to a warrant that merely authorized the seizure of books, pamphlets, and other written instruments "concerning the Communist Party of Texas."

---

[139] Heller v. New York, 413 U.S. 483 (1973).

[140] Id. at 492–93. *But cf.* New York v. P.J. Video, Inc., 475 U.S. 868, 875 n.6 (1986), rejecting the defendant's assertion, based on *Heller*, that only a single copy rather than all copies of allegedly obscene movies should have been seized pursuant to warrant.

[141] Roaden v. Kentucky, 413 U.S. 496 (1973). *See also* Lo-Ji Sales v. New York, 442 U.S. 319 (1979); Walter v. United States, 447 U.S. 649 (1980). These special constraints are inapplicable when obscene materials are purchased, and there is consequently no Fourth Amendment search or seizure. Maryland v. Macon, 472 U.S. 463 (1985).

[142] Lee Art Theatre, Inc. v. Virginia, 392 U.S. 636, 637 (1968) (per curiam).

[143] New York v. P.J. Video, Inc., 475 U.S. 868, 873–74 (1986) (quoting Marcus v. Search Warrant, 367 U.S. 717, 732 (1961)).

[144] New York v. P.J. Video, Inc., 475 U.S. 868, 875 n.6 (1986).

[145] 379 U.S. 476 (1965).

"[T]he constitutional requirement that warrants must particularly describe the 'things to be seized' is to be accorded the most scrupulous exactitude when the 'things' are books, and the basis for their seizure is the ideas which they contain. . . . No less a standard could be faithful to First Amendment freedoms." [146]

However, the First Amendment does not bar the issuance or execution of a warrant to search a newsroom to obtain photographs of demonstrators who had injured several policemen, although the Court appeared to suggest that a magistrate asked to issue such a warrant should guard against interference with press freedoms through limits on type, scope, and intrusiveness of the search.[147]

Property Subject to Seizure.—There has never been any doubt that search warrants could be issued for the seizure of contraband and the fruits and instrumentalities of crime.[148] But, in *Gouled v. United States*,[149] a unanimous Court limited the classes of property subject to seizures to these three and refused to permit a seizure of "mere evidence," in this instance papers of the defendant that were to be used as evidence against him at trial. The Court recognized that there was "no special sanctity in papers, as distinguished from other forms of property, to render them immune from search and seizure," [150] but their character as evidence rendered them immune. This immunity "was based upon the dual, related premises that historically the right to search for and seize property depended upon the assertion by the Government of a valid claim of superior interest, and that it was not enough that the purpose of the search and seizure was to obtain evidence to use in apprehending and convicting criminals." [151] More evaded than followed, the

---

[146] 379 U.S. at 485–86. *See also* Marcus v. Search Warrant, 367 U.S. 717, 723 (1961).

[147] Zurcher v. Stanford Daily, 436 U.S. 547 (1978). *See id.* at 566 (containing suggestion mentioned in text), and *id.* at 566 (Justice Powell concurring) (more expressly adopting that position). In the Privacy Protection Act, Pub. L. 96–440, 94 Stat. 1879 (1980), 42 U.S.C. § 2000aa, Congress provided extensive protection against searches and seizures not only of the news media and news people but also of others engaged in disseminating communications to the public, unless there is probable cause to believe the person protecting the materials has committed or is committing the crime to which the materials relate.

[148] United States v. Lefkowitz, 285 U.S. 452, 465–66 (1932). Of course, evidence seizable under warrant is subject to seizure without a warrant in circumstances in which warrantless searches are justified.

[149] 255 U.S. 298 (1921). United States v. Lefkowitz, 285 U.S. 452 (1932), applied the rule in a warrantless search of premises. The rule apparently never applied in case of a search of the person. *Cf.* Schmerber v. California, 384 U.S. 757 (1966).

[150] Gouled v. United States, 255 U.S. 298, 306 (1921).

[151] Warden v. Hayden, 387 U.S. 294, 303 (1967). *See* Gouled v. United States, 255 U.S. 298, 309 (1921). The holding was derived from dicta in Boyd v. United States, 116 U.S. 616, 624–29 (1886).

"mere evidence" rule was overturned in 1967.[152] It is now settled that such evidentiary items as fingerprints,[153] blood,[154] urine samples,[155] fingernail and skin scrapings,[156] voice and handwriting exemplars,[157] conversations,[158] and other demonstrative evidence may be obtained through the warrant process or without a warrant where "special needs" of government are shown.[159]

However, some medically assisted bodily intrusions have been held impermissible, *e.g.*, forcible administration of an emetic to induce vomiting,[160] and surgery under general anesthetic to remove a bullet lodged in a suspect's chest.[161] Factors to be weighed in determining which medical tests and procedures are reasonable include the extent to which the procedure threatens the individual's safety or health, "the extent of the intrusion upon the individual's dignitary interests in personal privacy and bodily integrity," and the importance of the evidence to the prosecution's case.[162]

In *Warden v. Hayden*,[163] Justice Brennan for the Court cautioned that the items there seized were not "'testimonial' or 'communicative' in nature, and their introduction therefore did not compel respondent to become a witness against himself in violation of

---

[152] Warden v. Hayden, 387 U.S. 294 (1967).

[153] Davis v. Mississippi, 394 U.S. 721 (1969).

[154] Schmerber v. California, 384 U.S. 757 (1966); Skinner v. Railway Labor Executives' Ass'n, 489 U.S. 602 (1989) (warrantless blood testing for drug use by railroad employee involved in accident).

[155] Skinner v. Railway Labor Executives' Ass'n, 489 U.S. 602 (1989) (warrantless drug testing of railroad employee involved in accident).

[156] Cupp v. Murphy, 412 U.S. 291 (1973) (sustaining warrantless taking of scrapings from defendant's fingernails at the station house, on the basis that it was a very limited intrusion and necessary to preserve evanescent evidence).

[157] United States v. Dionisio, 410 U.S. 1 (1973); United States v. Mara, 410 U.S. 19 (1973) (both sustaining grand jury subpoenas to produce voice and handwriting exemplars, as no reasonable expectation of privacy exists with respect to those items).

[158] Berger v. New York, 388 U.S. 41, 44 n.2 (1967). *See also* id. at 97 n.4, 107–08 (Justices Harlan and White concurring), 67 (Justice Douglas concurring).

[159] Another important result of Warden v. Hayden is that third parties not suspected of culpability in crime are subject to the issuance and execution of warrants for searches and seizures of evidence. Zurcher v. Stanford Daily, 436 U.S. 547, 553–60 (1978). Justice Stevens argued for a stiffer standard for issuance of warrants to nonsuspects, requiring in order to invade their privacy a showing that they would not comply with a less intrusive method, such as a subpoena. Id. at 577 (dissenting).

[160] Rochin v. California, 342 U.S. 165 (1952).

[161] Winston v. Lee, 470 U.S. 753 (1985).

[162] Winston v. Lee, 470 U.S. 753, 761–63 (1985). Chief Justice Burger concurred on the basis of his reading of the Court's opinion "as not preventing detention of an individual if there are reasonable grounds to believe that natural bodily functions will disclose the presence of contraband materials secreted internally." Id. at 767. *Cf.* United States v. Montoya de Hernandez, 473 U.S. 531 (1985).

[163] 387 U.S. 294, 302–03 (1967). Seizure of a diary was at issue in Hill v. California, 401 U.S. 797, 805 (1971), but it had not been raised in the state courts and was deemed waived.

the Fifth Amendment. . . . This case thus does not require that we consider whether there are items of evidential value whose very nature precludes them from being the object of a reasonable search and seizure." This merging of Fourth and Fifth Amendment considerations derived from *Boyd v. United States*,[164] the first case in which the Supreme Court considered at length the meaning of the Fourth Amendment. *Boyd* was a quasi-criminal proceeding for the forfeiture of goods alleged to have been imported in violation of law, and concerned a statute that authorized court orders to require defendants to produce any document that might "tend to prove any allegation made by the United States."[165] The entire Court agreed that there was a self-incrimination problem, but Justice Bradley for a majority of the Justices also used the Fourth Amendment.

Although the statute did not authorize a search but instead compelled the production of documents, the Justice concluded that the law was well within the restrictions of the Search and Seizure Clause.[166] With this point established, the Justice relied on Lord Camden's opinion in *Entick v. Carrington*[167] for the proposition that seizure of items to be used as evidence only was impermissible. Justice Bradley announced that the "essence of the offence" committed by the government against Boyd "is not the breaking of his doors, and the rummaging of his drawers . . . but it is the invasion of his indefeasible right of personal security, personal liberty and private property. . . . Breaking into a house and opening boxes and drawers are circumstances of aggravation; but any forcible and compulsory extortion of a man's own testimony or of his private papers to be used as evidence to convict him of crime or to forfeit his goods, is within the condemnation of that judgment. In this regard the Fourth and Fifth Amendments run almost into each other."[168]

Although it may be doubtful that the equation of search warrants with subpoenas and other compulsory process ever really amounted to much of a limitation,[169] the Court currently dispenses with any theory of "convergence" of the two amendments.[170] Thus, in *Andresen v. Maryland*,[171] police executed a warrant to search defendant's offices for specified documents pertaining to a fraudulent sale of land, and the Court sustained the admission of the papers

---

[164] 116 U.S. 616 (1886).

[165] Act of June 22, 1874, § 5, 18 Stat. 187.

[166] Boyd v. United States, 116 U.S. 616, 622 (1886).

[167] Howell's State Trials 1029, 95 Eng. Rep. 807 (1765).

[168] Boyd v. United States, 116 U.S. 616, 630 (1886).

[169] *E.g.*, Oklahoma Press Publishing Co. v. Walling, 327 U.S. 186, 209–09 (1946).

[170] Andresen v. Maryland, 427 U.S. 463 (1976); Fisher v. United States, 425 U.S. 391, 405–14 (1976). *Fisher* states that "the precise claim sustained in *Boyd* would now be rejected for reasons not there considered." Id. at 408.

[171] 427 U.S. 463 (1976).

discovered as evidence at his trial. The Fifth Amendment was inapplicable, the Court held, because there had been no compulsion of defendant to produce or to authenticate the documents.[172] As for the Fourth Amendment, because the "business records" seized were evidence of criminal acts, they were properly seizable under the rule of *Warden v. Hayden*; the fact that they were "testimonial" in nature (records in the defendant's handwriting) was irrelevant.[173] Acknowledging that "there are grave dangers inherent in executing a warrant authorizing a search and seizure of a person's papers," the Court observed that, although some "innocuous documents" would have to be examined to ascertain which papers were to be seized, authorities, just as with electronic "seizures" of telephone conversations, "must take care to assure that [searches] are conducted in a manner that minimizes unwarranted intrusions upon privacy."[174]

Although *Andresen* was concerned with business records, its discussion seemed equally applicable to "personal" papers, such as diaries and letters, as to which a much greater interest in privacy exists. The question of the propriety of seizure of such papers continues to be the subject of reservation in opinions,[175] but it is far from clear that the Court would accept any such exception should the issue be presented.[176]

Execution of Warrants.—The Fourth Amendment's "general touchstone of reasonableness . . . governs the method of execution of the warrant."[177] Until recently, however, most such issues have been dealt with by statute and rule.[178] It was a rule at common law that before an officer could break and enter he must give notice of his office, authority, and purpose and must in effect be refused admittance,[179] and until recently this has been a statutory

---

[172] 427 U.S. at 470–77.

[173] 427 U.S. at 478–84.

[174] 427 U.S. at 482, n.11. Minimization, as required under federal law, has not proved to be a significant limitation. Scott v. United States, 425 U.S. 917 (1976).

[175] *E.g.*, United States v. Miller, 425 U.S. 435, 440, 444 (1976); Fisher v. United States, 425 U.S. 391, 401 (1976); California Bankers Ass'n v. Shultz, 416 U.S. 21, 78–79 (1974) (Justice Powell concurring).

[176] *See,* Note, *Formalism, Legal Realism, and Constitutionally Protected Privacy Under the Fourth and Fifth Amendments,* 90 HARV. L. REV. 945 (1977).

[177] United States v. Ramirez, 523 U.S. 65, 71 (1998).

[178] Rule 41(c), Federal Rules of Criminal Procedure, provides, inter alia, that the warrant shall command its execution in the daytime, unless the magistrate "for reasonable cause shown" directs in the warrant that it be served at some other time. *See* Jones v. United States, 357 U.S. 493, 498–500 (1958); Gooding v. United States, 416 U.S. 430 (1974). A separate statutory rule applies to narcotics cases. 21 U.S.C. § 879(a).

[179] *Semayne's Case*, 5 Coke's Rep. 91a, 77 Eng. Rep. 194 (K.B. 1604).

requirement in the federal system [180] and generally in the states. In *Ker v. California*,[181] the Court considered the rule of announcement as a constitutional requirement, although a majority there found circumstances justifying entry without announcement.

In *Wilson v. Arkansas*,[182] the Court determined that the common law "knock and announce" rule is an element of the Fourth Amendment reasonableness inquiry. The rule is merely a presumption, however, that yields under various circumstances, including those posing a threat of physical violence to officers, those in which a prisoner has escaped and taken refuge in his dwelling, and those in which officers have reason to believe that destruction of evidence is likely. The test, articulated two years later in *Richards v. Wisconsin*,[183] is whether police have "a reasonable suspicion that knocking and announcing their presence, under the particular circumstances, would be dangerous or futile, or that it would inhibit the effective investigation of the crime." In *Richards*, the Court held that there is no blanket exception to the rule whenever officers are executing a search warrant in a felony drug investigation; instead, a case-by-case analysis is required to determine whether no-knock entry is justified under the circumstances.[184] Similarly, if officers choose to knock and announce before searching for drugs, circumstances may justify forced entry if there is not a prompt response.[185] Recent federal laws providing for the issuance of warrants authorizing in certain circumstances "no-knock" entries to execute warrants will no doubt present the Court with opportunities to explore the configurations of the rule of announcement.[186] A statute regulating the expiration of a warrant and issuance of another "should

---

[180] 18 U.S.C. § 3109. *See* Miller v. United States, 357 U.S. 301 (1958); Wong Sun v. United States, 371 U.S. 471 (1963).

[181] 374 U.S. 23 (1963). *Ker* was an arrest warrant case, but no reason appears for differentiating search warrants. Eight Justices agreed that federal standards should govern and that the rule of announcement was of constitutional stature, but they divided 4-to-4 whether entry in this case had been pursuant to a valid exception. Justice Harlan who had dissented from the federal standards issue joined the four finding a justifiable exception to carry the result.

[182] 514 U.S. 927 (1995).

[183] 520 U.S. 385, 394 (1997).

[184] The fact that officers may have to destroy property in order to conduct a no-knock entry has no bearing on the reasonableness of their decision not to knock and announce. United States v. Ramirez, 523 U.S. 65 (1998).

[185] United States v. Banks, 540 U.S. 31 (2003) (forced entry was permissible after officers executing a warrant to search for drugs knocked, announced "police search warrant," and waited 15–20 seconds with no response).

[186] In narcotics cases, magistrates are authorized to issue "no-knock" warrants if they find there is probable cause to believe (1) the property sought may, and if notice is given, will be easily and quickly destroyed or (2) giving notice will endanger the life or safety of the executing officer or another person. 21 U.S.C. § 879(b). *See also* D.C. Code, § 23–591.

be liberally construed in favor of the individual."[187] Similarly, just as the existence of probable cause must be established by fresh facts, so the execution of the warrant should be done in timely fashion so as to ensure so far as possible the continued existence of probable cause.[188]

Because police actions in execution of a warrant must be related to the objectives of the authorized intrusion, and because privacy of the home lies at the core of the Fourth Amendment, police officers violate the Amendment by bringing members of the media or other third parties into a home during execution of a warrant if presence of those persons was not in aid of execution of the warrant.[189]

In executing a warrant for a search of premises and of named persons on the premises, police officers may not automatically search someone else found on the premises.[190] If they can articulate some reasonable basis for fearing for their safety they may conduct a "patdown" of the person, but in order to search they must have probable cause particularized with respect to that person. However, in *Michigan v. Summers*,[191] the Court held that officers arriving to execute a warrant for the search of a house could detain, without being required to articulate any reasonable basis and necessarily therefore without probable cause, the owner or occupant of the house, whom they encountered on the front porch leaving the premises. The Court determined that such a detention, which was "substantially less intrusive" than an arrest, was justified because of the law enforcement interests in minimizing the risk of harm to officers, facilitating entry and conduct of the search, and preventing flight in the event incriminating evidence is found.[192] For the same

---

[187] Sgro v. United States, 287 U.S. 206 (1932).

[188] Sgro v. United States, 287 U.S. 206 (1932).

[189] Wilson v. Layne, 526 U.S. 603 (1999). *Accord*, Hanlon v. Berger, 526 U.S. 808 (1999) (media camera crew "ride-along" with Fish and Wildlife Service agents executing a warrant to search respondent's ranch for evidence of illegal taking of wildlife).

[190] Ybarra v. Illinois, 444 U.S. 85 (1979) (patron in a bar), relying on and reaffirming United States v. Di Re, 332 U.S. 581 (1948) (occupant of vehicle may not be searched merely because there are grounds to search the automobile). *But see* Maryland v. Pringle, 540 U.S. 366 (2003) (distinguishing *Ybarra* on basis that passengers in car often have "common enterprise," and noting that the tip in *Di Re* implicated only the driver.

[191] 452 U.S. 692 (1981).

[192] 452 U.S. at 701–06. *Ybarra* was distinguished on the basis of its greater intrusiveness and the lack of sufficient connection with the premises. Id. at 695 n.4. By the time Summers was searched, police had probable cause to do so. Id. at 695. The warrant here was for contraband, id. at 701, and a different rule may apply with respect to warrants for other evidence, id. at 705 n.20. In Los Angeles County v. Rettele, 550 U.S. 609 (2007), the Court found no Fourth Amendment violation where deputies did not know that the suspects had sold the house that the deputies

reasons, officers may use "reasonable force," including handcuffs, to effectuate a detention.[193] Also, under some circumstances, officers may search premises on the mistaken but reasonable belief that the premises are described in an otherwise valid warrant.[194]

Limits on detention incident to a search were addressed in *Bailey v. United States,* a case in which an occupant exited his residence and traveled some distance before being stopped and detained.[195] The *Bailey* Court held that the detention was not constitutionally sustainable under the rule announced in *Summers.*[196] According to the Court, application of the categorical exception to probable cause requirements for detention incident to a search is determined by spatial proximity, that is, whether the occupant is found "within the immediate vicinity of the premises to be searched,"[197] and not by temporal proximity, that is, whether the occupant is detained "as soon as reasonably practicable" consistent with safety and security. In so holding, the Court reasoned that limiting the *Summers* rule to the area within which an occupant poses a real threat ensures that the scope of the rule regarding detention incident to a search is confined to its underlying justification.[198]

Although, for purposes of execution, as for many other matters, there is little difference between search warrants and arrest warrants, one notable difference is that the possession of a valid arrest warrant cannot authorize authorities to enter the home of a third party looking for the person named in the warrant; in order to do

---

had a warrant to search. The deputies entered the house and found the new owners, of a different race from the suspects, sleeping in the nude. The deputies held the new owners at gunpoint for one to two minutes without allowing them to dress or cover themselves. As for the difference in race, the Court noted that, "[w]hen the deputies ordered [Caucasian] respondents from their bed, they had no way of knowing whether the African-American suspects were elsewhere in the house." Id. at 613. As for not allowing the new owners to dress or cover themselves, the Court quoted its statement in Michigan v. Summers that "[t]he risk of harm to both the police and the occupants is minimized if the officers routinely exercise unquestioned command of the situation." Id. at 1993 (quoting 452 U.S. at 702–03).

[193] Muehler v. Mena, 544 U.S. 93, 98–99 (2005) (also upholding questioning the handcuffed detainee about her immigration status).

[194] Maryland v. Garrison, 480 U.S. 79 (1987) (officers reasonably believed there was only one "third floor apartment" in city row house when in fact there were two).

[195] 568 U.S. ___, No. 11–770, slip op. (2013). In *Bailey,* the police obtained a warrant to search Bailey's residence for firearms and drugs *Id.* at 2. Meanwhile, detectives staked out the residence, saw Bailey leave and drive away, and then called in a search team. *Id.* While the search was proceeding, the detectives tailed Bailey for about a mile before stopping and detaining him. *Id.* at 2–3.

[196] As an alternative ground, the district court had found that stopping Bailey was lawful as an investigatory stop under *Terry v. Ohio,* 392 U.S. 1, 20 (1968), but the Supreme Court offered no opinion on whether, assuming the stop was valid under *Terry,* the resulting interaction between law enforcement and Bailey could independently have justified Bailey's detention. *Bailey,* slip op. at 14.

[197] *Bailey,* slip op. at 13–14.

[198] *Id.* at 13.

that, they need a search warrant signifying that a magistrate has determined that there is probable cause to believe the person named is on the premises.[199]

Valid Searches and Seizures Without Warrants

Although the Supreme Court stresses the importance of warrants and has repeatedly referred to searches without warrants as "exceptional,"[200] it appears that the greater number of searches, as well as the vast number of arrests, take place without warrants. The Reporters of the American Law Institute Project on a Model Code of Pre-Arraignment Procedure have noted "their conviction that, as a practical matter, searches without warrant and incidental to arrest have been up to this time, and may remain, of greater practical importance" than searches pursuant to warrants. "[T]he evidence on hand . . . compel[s] the conclusion that searches under warrants have played a comparatively minor part in law enforcement, except in connection with narcotics and gambling laws."[201] Nevertheless, the Court frequently asserts that "the most basic constitutional rule in this area is that 'searches conducted outside the judicial process, without prior approval by judge or magistrate, are *per se* unreasonable under the Fourth Amendment—subject only to a few specially established and well-delineated exceptions.'"[202] The exceptions are said to be "jealously and carefully drawn,"[203] and there must be "a showing by those who seek exemption . . . that the exigencies of the situation made that course imperative."[204] Although the record indicates an effort to categorize the exceptions, the number and breadth of those exceptions have been growing.

Detention Short of Arrest: Stop and Frisk.—Arrests are subject to the requirements of the Fourth Amendment, but the courts have followed the common law in upholding the right of police offi-

---

[199] Steagald v. United States, 451 U.S. 204 (1981). An arrest warrant is a necessary and sufficient authority to enter a suspect's home to arrest him. Payton v. New York, 445 U.S. 573 (1980).

[200] *E.g.*, Johnson v. United States, 333 U.S. 10, 14 (1948); McDonald v. United States, 335 U.S. 451, 453 (1948); Camara v. Municipal Court, 387 U.S. 523, 528–29 (1967); G.M. Leasing Corp. v. United States, 429 U.S. 338, 352–53, 355 (1977).

[201] American Law Institute, A Model Code of Pre-Arraignment Procedure, Tent. Draft No. 3 (Philadelphia: 1970), xix.

[202] Coolidge v. New Hampshire, 403 U.S. 443, 454–55 (1971) (quoting Katz v. United States, 389 U.S. 347, 357 (1967)); G.M. Leasing Corp. v. United States, 429 U.S. 338, 352–53, 358 (1977).

[203] Jones v. United States, 357 U.S. 493, 499 (1958).

[204] McDonald v. United States, 335 U.S. 451, 456 (1948). In general, with regard to exceptions to the warrant clause, conduct must be tested by the reasonableness standard enunciated by the first clause of the Amendment, Terry v. Ohio, 392 U.S. 1, 20 (1968). The Court's development of its privacy expectation tests, discussed under "The Interest Protected," *supra*, substantially changed the content of that standard.

cers to take a person into custody without a warrant if they have probable cause to believe that the person to be arrested has committed a felony or a misdemeanor in their presence.[205] Probable cause is, of course, the same standard required to be met in the issuance of an arrest warrant, and must be satisfied by conditions existing prior to the police officer's stop, what is discovered thereafter not sufficing to establish probable cause retroactively.[206] There are, however, instances when a police officer's suspicions will have been aroused by someone's conduct or manner, but probable cause for placing such a person under arrest will be lacking.[207] In *Terry v. Ohio*,[208] the Court, with only Justice Douglas dissenting, approved an on-the-street investigation by a police officer that involved "patting down" the subject of the investigation for weapons.

Terry arose when a police officer observed three individuals engaging in conduct which appeared to him, on the basis of training and experience, to be the "casing" of a store for a likely armed robbery. Upon approaching the men, identifying himself, and not receiving prompt identification, the officer seized one of the men, patted the exterior of his clothes, and discovered a gun. Chief Justice Warren for the Court wrote that the Fourth Amendment was applicable "whenever a police officer accosts an individual and restrains his freedom to walk away."[209] Because the warrant clause is necessarily and practically of no application to the type of on-the-street encounter present in *Terry*, the Chief Justice continued, the question was whether the policeman's actions were reasonable. The test of reasonableness in this sort of situation is whether the police officer can point to "specific and articulable facts which, taken together with rational inferences from those facts," would lead a neutral magistrate on review to conclude that a man of reasonable caution would be warranted in believing that possible criminal behavior was at hand and that both an investigative stop and a "frisk" was required.[210] Because the conduct witnessed by the police officer reasonably led him to believe that an armed robbery was in prospect, he was as reasonably led to believe that the men were armed and probably dangerous and that his safety required a "frisk." Because the object of the "frisk" is the discovery of dangerous weapons, "it must therefore be confined in scope to an intrusion reasonably de-

---

[205] United States v. Watson, 423 U.S. 411 (1976).

[206] Henry v. United States, 361 U.S. 98 (1959); Johnson v. United States, 333 U.S. 10, 16–17 (1948); Sibron v. New York, 392 U.S. 40, 62–63 (1968).

[207] "The police may not arrest upon mere suspicion but only on 'probable cause.'" Mallory v. United States, 354 U.S. 449, 454 (1957).

[208] 392 U.S. 1 (1968).

[209] 392 U.S. at 16. *See* id. at 16–20.

[210] 392 U.S. at 20, 21, 22.

signed to discover guns, knives, clubs, or other hidden instruments for the assault of the police officer."[211]

In a later case, the Court held that an officer may seize an object if, in the course of a weapons frisk, "plain touch" reveals the presence of the object, and the officer has probable cause to believe it is contraband.[212] The Court viewed the situation as analogous to that covered by the "plain view" doctrine: obvious contraband may be seized, but a search may not be expanded to determine whether an object is contraband.[213] Also impermissible is physical manipulation, without reasonable suspicion, of a bus passenger's carry-on luggage stored in an overhead compartment.[214]

Terry did not rule on a host of problems, including the grounds that could permissibly lead an officer to momentarily stop a person on the street or elsewhere in order to ask questions rather than frisk for weapons, the right of the stopped individual to refuse to cooperate, and the permissible response of the police to that refusal. The Court provided a partial answer in 2004, when it upheld a state law that required a suspect to disclose his name in the course of a valid *Terry* stop.[215] Questions about a suspect's identity "are a routine and accepted part of many *Terry* stops," the Court explained.[216]

---

[211] 392 U.S. at 23–27, 29. *See also* Sibron v. New York, 392 U.S. 40 (1968) (after policeman observed defendant speak with several known narcotics addicts, he approached him and placed his hand in defendant's pocket, thus discovering narcotics; this was impermissible, because he lacked a reasonable basis for the frisk and in any event his search exceeded the permissible scope of a weapons frisk); Adams v. Williams, 407 U.S. 143 (1972) (stop and frisk based on informer's in-person tip that defendant was sitting in an identified parked car, visible to informer and officer, in a high crime area at 2 a.m., with narcotics and a gun at his waist); Pennsylvania v. Mimms, 434 U.S. 106 (1977) (after validly stopping car, officer required defendant to get out of car, observed bulge under his jacket, and frisked him and seized weapon; while officer did not suspect driver of crime or have an articulable basis for safety fears, safety considerations justified his requiring driver to leave car); Maryland v. Wilson, 519 U.S. 408, 413 (1997) (after validly stopping car, officer may order passengers as well as driver out of car; "the same weighty interest in officer safety is present regardless of whether the occupant of the stopped car is a driver or passenger"); Arizona v. Johnson, 129 S. Ct. 781, 786 (2009) (after validly stopping car, officer may frisk (patdown for weapons) both the driver and any passengers whom he reasonably concludes "might be armed and presently dangerous").

[212] Minnesota v. Dickerson, 508 U.S. 366 (1993).

[213] 508 U.S. at 375, 378–79. In *Dickerson* the Court held that seizure of a small plastic container that the officer felt in the suspect's pocket was not justified; the officer should not have continued the search, manipulating the container with his fingers, after determining that no weapon was present.

[214] Bond v. United States, 529 U.S. 334 (2000) (bus passenger has reasonable expectation that, although other passengers might handle his bag in order to make room for their own, they will not "feel the bag in an exploratory manner").

[215] Hiibel v. Sixth Judicial Dist. Ct., 542 U.S. 177 (2004).

[216] 542 U.S. at 186.

After *Terry*, the standard for stops for investigative purposes evolved into one of "reasonable suspicion of criminal activity." That test permits some stops and questioning without probable cause in order to allow police officers to explore the foundations of their suspicions.[217] Although it did not elaborate a set of rules to govern the application of the tests, the Court was initially restrictive in recognizing permissible bases for reasonable suspicion.[218] Extensive intrusions on individual privacy, *e.g.*, transportation to the station house for interrogation and fingerprinting, were invalidated in the absence of probable cause,[219] although the Court has held that an uncorroborated, anonymous tip is insufficient basis for a *Terry* stop, and that there is no "firearms" exception to the reasonable suspicion requirement.[220] More recently, however, the Court has taken less restrictive approaches.[221]

It took the Court some time to settle on a test for when a "seizure" has occurred, and the Court has recently modified its approach. The issue is of some importance, since it is at this point that Fourth Amendment protections take hold. The *Terry* Court rec-

---

[217] In United States v. Cortez, 449 U.S. 411 (1981), a unanimous Court attempted to capture the "elusive concept" of the basis for permitting a stop. Officers must have "articulable reasons" or "founded suspicions," derived from the totality of the circumstances. "Based upon that whole picture the detaining officer must have a particularized and objective basis for suspecting the particular person stopped of criminal activity." Id. at 417–18. The inquiry is thus quite fact-specific. In the anonymous tip context, the same basic approach requiring some corroboration applies regardless of whether the standard is probable cause or reasonable suspicion; the difference is that less information, or less reliable information, can satisfy the lower standard. Alabama v. White, 496 U.S. 325 (1990).

[218] *E.g.*, Brown v. Texas, 443 U.S. 47 (1979) (individual's presence in high crime area gave officer no articulable basis to suspect him of crime); Delaware v. Prouse, 440 U.S. 648 (1979) (reasonable suspicion of a license or registration violation is necessary to authorize automobile stop; random stops impermissible); United States v. Brignoni-Ponce, 422 U.S. 873 (1975) (officers could not justify random automobile stop solely on basis of Mexican appearance of occupants); Reid v. Georgia, 448 U.S. 438 (1980) (no reasonable suspicion for airport stop based on appearance that suspect and another passenger were trying to conceal the fact that they were traveling together). *But cf.* United States v. Martinez-Fuerte, 428 U.S. 543 (1976) (halting vehicles at fixed checkpoints to question occupants as to citizenship and immigration status permissible, even if officers should act on basis of appearance of occupants).

[219] Davis v. Mississippi, 394 U.S. 721 (1969); Dunaway v. New York, 442 U.S. 200 (1979). Illinois v. Wardlow, 528 U.S. 119 (2000) (unprovoked flight from high crime area upon sight of police produces "reasonable suspicion").

[220] Florida v. J.L., 529 U.S. 266 (2000) (reasonable suspicion requires that a tip be reliable in its assertion of illegality, not merely in its identification of someone).

[221] *See, e.g.*, Prado Navarette v. California, 572 U.S. ___, No. 12–9490, slip op. (2014) (anonymous 911 call reporting an erratic swerve by a particular truck traveling in a particular direction held to be sufficient to justify stop); United States v. Sokolow, 490 U.S. 1, 9 (1989) (airport stop based on drug courier profile may rely on a combination of factors that individually may be "quite consistent with innocent travel"); United States v. Hensley, 469 U.S. 221 (1985) (reasonable suspicion to stop a motorist may be based on a "wanted flyer" as long as issuance of the flyer has been based on reasonable suspicion).

ognized in dictum that "not all personal intercourse between police-men and citizens involves 'seizures' of persons," and suggested that "[o]nly when the officer, by means of physical force or show of authority, has in some way restrained the liberty of a citizen may we conclude that a 'seizure' has occurred." [222] Years later Justice Stewart proposed a similar standard—that a person has been seized "only if, in view of all of the circumstances surrounding the incident, a reasonable person would have believed that he was not free to leave." [223] A majority of the Justices subsequently endorsed this reasonable perception standard [224] and applied it in several cases in which admissibility of evidence turned on whether a seizure of the person not justified by probable cause or reasonable suspicion had occurred prior to the uncovering of the evidence. No seizure occurred, for example, when INS agents seeking to identify illegal aliens conducted workforce surveys within a garment factory; while some agents were positioned at exits, others systematically moved through the factory and questioned employees.[225] This brief questioning, even with blocked exits, amounted to "classic consensual encounters rather than Fourth Amendment seizures." [226] The Court also ruled that no seizure had occurred when police in a squad car drove alongside a suspect who had turned and run down the sidewalk when he saw the squad car approach. Under the circumstances (no siren, flashing lights, display of a weapon, or blocking of the suspect's path), the Court concluded, the police conduct "would not have communicated to the reasonable person an attempt to capture or otherwise intrude upon [one's] freedom of movement." [227]

Soon after, however, the Court departed from the *Mendenhall* reasonable-perception standard and adopted a more formalistic approach, holding that an actual chase with evident intent to capture did not amount to a "seizure" because the suspect had not complied with the officer's order to halt. The Court in *California v. Hodari D.* wrote that *Mendenhall* stated a "necessary" but not a "sufficient" condition for a seizure of the person through show of authority.[228] A Fourth Amendment "seizure" of the person, the Court determined, is the same as a common law arrest; there must be either application of physical force (or the laying on of hands), or submis-

---

[222] 392 U.S. at 19, n.16.

[223] United States v. Mendenhall, 446 U.S. 544, 554 (1980).

[224] *See, e.g.*, Florida v. Royer, 460 U.S. 491 (1983), in which there was no opinion of the Court, but in which the test was used by the plurality of four, id. at 502, and also endorsed by dissenting Justice Blackmun, id. at 514.

[225] INS v. Delgado, 466 U.S. 210 (1984).

[226] 466 U.S. at 221.

[227] Michigan v. Chesternut, 486 U.S. 567, 575 (1988).

[228] 499 U.S. 621, 628 (1991). As in Michigan v. Chesternut, *supra*, the suspect dropped incriminating evidence while being chased.

sion to the assertion of authority.[229] Indications are, however, that *Hodari D.* did not signal the end of the reasonable perception standard, but merely carved an exception applicable to chases and perhaps other encounters between suspects and police.

Later in the same term the Court ruled that the *Mendenhall* "free-to-leave" inquiry was misplaced in the context of a police sweep of a bus, but that a modified reasonable perception approach still governed.[230] In conducting a bus sweep, aimed at detecting illegal drugs and their couriers, police officers typically board a bus during a stopover at a terminal and ask to inspect tickets, identification, and sometimes luggage of selected passengers. The Court did not focus on whether an "arrest" had taken place, as adherence to the *Hodari D.* approach would have required, but instead suggested that the appropriate inquiry is "whether a reasonable person would feel free to decline the officers' requests or otherwise terminate the encounter."[231] "When the person is seated on a bus and has no desire to leave," the Court explained, "the degree to which a reasonable person would feel that he or she could leave is not an accurate measure of the coercive effect of the encounter."[232]

A *Terry* search need not be limited to a stop and frisk of the person, but may extend as well to a protective search of the passenger compartment of a car if an officer possesses "a reasonable belief, based on specific and articulable facts . . . that the suspect is dangerous and . . . may gain immediate control of weapons."[233] How lengthy a *Terry* detention may be varies with the circumstances. In approving a 20-minute detention of a driver made necessary by the driver's own evasion of drug agents and a state police decision to

---

[229] Adherence to this approach would effectively nullify the Court's earlier position that Fourth Amendment protections extend to "seizures that involve only a brief detention short of traditional arrest." United States v. Brignoni-Ponce, 422 U.S. 873, 878 (1975), *quoted in* INS v. Delgado, 466 U.S. 210, 215 (1984).

[230] Florida v. Bostick, 501 U.S. 429 (1991).

[231] 501 U.S. at 436.

[232] 501 U.S. at 436. The Court asserted that the case was "analytically indistinguishable from *Delgado.* Like the workers in that case [subjected to the INS 'survey' at their workplace], Bostick's freedom of movement was restricted by a factor independent of police conduct—*i.e.*, by his being a passenger on a bus." Id. *See also* United States v. Drayton, 536 U.S. 194 (2002), applying *Bostick* to uphold a bus search in which one officer stationed himself in the front of the bus and one in the rear, while a third officer worked his way from rear to front, questioning passengers individually. Under these circumstances, and following the arrest of his traveling companion, the defendant had consented to the search of his person.

[233] Michigan v. Long, 463 U.S. 1032 (1983) (suspect appeared to be under the influence of drugs, officer spied hunting knife exposed on floor of front seat and searched remainder of passenger compartment). Similar reasoning has been applied to uphold a "protective sweep" of a home in which an arrest is made if arresting officers have a reasonable belief that the area swept may harbor another individual posing a danger to the officers or to others. Maryland v. Buie, 494 U.S. 325 (1990).

hold the driver until the agents could arrive on the scene, the Court indicated that it is "appropriate to examine whether the police diligently pursued a means of investigation that was likely to confirm or dispel their suspicions quickly, during which time it was necessary to detain the defendant."[234]

Similar principles govern detention of luggage at airports in order to detect the presence of drugs; *Terry* "limitations applicable to investigative detentions of the person should define the permissible scope of an investigative detention of the person's luggage on less than probable cause."[235] The general rule is that "when an officer's observations lead him reasonably to believe that a traveler is carrying luggage that contains narcotics, the principles of *Terry* . . . would permit the officer to detain the luggage briefly to investigate the circumstances that aroused his suspicion, provided that the investigative detention is properly limited in scope."[236] Seizure of luggage for an expeditious "canine sniff" by a dog trained to detect narcotics can satisfy this test even though seizure of luggage is in effect detention of the traveler, since the procedure results in "limited disclosure," impinges only slightly on a traveler's privacy interest in the contents of personal luggage, and does not constitute a search within the meaning of the Fourth Amendment.[237] By contrast, taking a suspect to an interrogation room on grounds short of probable cause, retaining his air ticket, and retrieving his luggage without his permission taints consent given under such circumstances to open the luggage, since by then the detention had exceeded the bounds of a permissible *Terry* investigative stop and amounted to an invalid arrest.[238] But the same requirements for brevity of de-

---

[234] United States v. Sharpe, 470 U.S. 675, 686 (1985). A more relaxed standard has been applied to detention of travelers at the border, the Court testing the reasonableness in terms of "the period of time necessary to either verify or dispel the suspicion." United States v. Montoya de Hernandez, 473 U.S. 531, 544 (1985) (approving warrantless detention for more than 24 hours of traveler suspected of alimentary canal drug smuggling).

[235] United States v. Place, 462 U.S. 696, 709 (1983).

[236] 462 U.S. at 706.

[237] 462 U.S. at 707. However, the search in *Place* was not expeditious, and hence exceeded Fourth Amendment bounds, when agents took 90 minutes to transport luggage to another airport for administration of the canine sniff. The length of a detention short of an arrest has similarly been a factor in other cases. *Compare* Illinois v. Caballes, 543 U.S. 405 (2005) (a canine sniff around the perimeter of a car following a routine traffic stop does not offend the Fourth Amendment if the duration of the stop is justified by the traffic offense) *with* Rodriguez v. United States, 575 U.S. ___, No. 13–9972, slip op. at 3, 5–6 (2015) (finding that the stop in question had been prolonged for seven to eight minutes beyond the time needed to resolve the traffic offense in order to conduct a canine sniff).

[238] Florida v. Royer, 460 U.S. 491 (1983). On this much the plurality opinion of Justice White (id. at 503), joined by three other Justices, and the concurring opinion of Justice Brennan (id. at 509) were in agreement.

tention and limited scope of investigation are apparently inapplicable to border searches of international travelers, the Court having approved a 24-hour detention of a traveler suspected of smuggling drugs in her alimentary canal.[239]

Search Incident to Arrest.—The common-law rule permitting searches of the person of an arrestee as an incident to the arrest has occasioned little controversy in the Court.[240] The Court has even upheld a search incident to an illegal (albeit not unconstitutional) arrest.[241] The dispute has centered around the scope of the search. Because it was the stated general rule that the scope of a warrantless search must be strictly tied to and justified by the circumstances that rendered its justification permissible, and because it was the rule that the justification of a search of the arrestee was to prevent destruction of evidence and to prevent access to a weapon,[242] it was argued to the court that a search of the person of the defendant arrested for a traffic offense, which discovered heroin in a crumpled cigarette package, was impermissible, because there could have been no destructible evidence relating to the offense for which he was arrested and no weapon could have been concealed in the cigarette package. The Court rejected this argument, ruling that "no additional justification" is required for a custodial arrest of a suspect based on probable cause.[243]

---

[239] United States v. Montoya de Hernandez, 473 U.S. 531 (1985).

[240] Weeks v. United States, 232 U.S. 383, 392 (1914); Carroll v. United States, 267 U.S. 132, 158 (1925); Agnello v. United States, 269 U.S. 20, 30 (1925).

[241] Virginia v. Moore, 128 S. Ct. 1598 (2008) (holding that, where an arrest for a minor offense is prohibited by state law, the arrest will not violate the Fourth Amendment if it was based on probable cause).

[242] Terry v. Ohio, 392 U.S. 1, 19 (1968); Chimel v. California, 395 U.S. 752, 762, 763 (1969). The Court, in *Birchfield v. North Dakota*, 579 U.S. ___, No. 14–1468, slip op. (2016), explained that the precedent allowing for a warrantless search of an arrestee in order to prevent the destruction of evidence applies to both evidence that could be actively destroyed by a suspect and to evidence that can be destroyed due to a natural process, such as the natural dissipation of the alcohol content in a suspect's blood. *Id.* at 30–31.

[243] United States v. Robinson, 414 U.S. 218, 235 (1973). *See also* id. at 237–38 (Justice Powell concurring). The Court applied the same rule in Gustafson v. Florida, 414 U.S. 260 (1973), involving a search of a motorist's person following his custodial arrest for an offense for which a citation would normally have issued. Unlike the situation in *Robinson*, police regulations did not require the *Gustafson* officer to take the suspect into custody, nor did a departmental policy guide the officer as to when to conduct a full search. The Court found these differences inconsequential, and left for another day the problem of pretextual arrests in order to obtain basis to search. Soon thereafter, the Court upheld conduct of a similar search at the place of detention, even after a time lapse between the arrest and search. United States v. Edwards, 415 U.S. 800 (1974).

The Court has disavowed a case-by-case evaluation of searches made post-arrest [244] and instead has embraced categorical evaluations as to post-arrest searches. Thus, in *Riley v. California*,[245] the Court declined to extend the holding of *United States v. Robinson* to the search of the digital data contained in a cell phone found on an arrestee. Specifically, the Court distinguished a search of cell phones, which contain vast quantities of personal data, from the limited physical search at issue in *Robinson*.[246] Focusing primarily on the rationale that searching cell phones would prevent the destruction of evidence, the government argued that cell phone data could be destroyed remotely or become encrypted by the passage of time. The Court, however, both discounted the prevalence of these events and the efficacy of warrantless searches to defeat them. Rather, the Court noted that other means existed besides a search of a cell phone to secure the data contained therein, including turning the phone off or placing the phone in a bag that isolates it from radio waves.[247] Because of the more substantial privacy interests at stake when digital data is involved in a search incident to an arrest and because of the availability of less intrusive alternatives to a warrantless search, the Court in *Riley* concluded that, as a "simple" categorical rule, before police can search a cell phone incident to an arrest, the police must "get a warrant."[248]

Two years after *Riley*, the Court again crafted a new brightline rule with respect to searches following an arrest in another "situation[] that could not have been envisioned when the Fourth Amendment was adopted."[249] In *Birchfield v. North Dakota*, the Court examined whether compulsory breath and blood tests administered in order to determine the blood alcohol concentration (BAC) of an automobile driver, following the arrest of that driver for suspected "drunk driving," are unreasonable under the search incident to arrest exception to the Fourth Amendment's warrant requirement.[250] In examining laws criminalizing the refusal to submit to either a breath or blood test, similar to *Riley*, the Court relied on a general

---

[244] In this vein, the search incident to arrest exception to the warrant requirement differs from other exceptions to the warrant requirement, such as the exigent circumstances exception. *See Birchfield*, slip op. at 15–16 (noting that while "other exceptions to the warrant requirement 'apply categorically'," the exigent circumstances exception to the warrant requirement applies on a case-by-case basis) (quoting Missouri v. McNeely, 569 U.S. ___, No. 11–1425, slip op. at 7 n.3 (2013)).

[245] 573 U.S. ___, No. 13–132, slip op. (2014).

[246] "Cell phones differ in both a quantitative and a qualitative sense from other objects that might be kept on an arrestee's person." *Id.* at 17.

[247] *Id.* at 14.

[248] *Id.* at 28.

[249] See *Birchfield*, slip op. at 19.

[250] *Id.* at 19.

balancing approach used to assess whether a given category of searches is reasonable, weighing the individual privacy interests implicated by such tests against any legitimate state interests.[251] With respect to *breath* tests, the *Birchfield* Court viewed the privacy intrusions posed by such tests as "almost negligible" in that a breath test is functionally equivalent to the process of using a straw to drink a beverage and yields a limited amount of useful information for law enforcement agents.[252] In contrast, the Court concluded that a mandatory *blood* test raised more serious privacy interests,[253] as blood tests pierce the skin, extract a part of the subject's body, and provide far more information than a breathalyzer test.[254] Turning to the state's interest in obtaining BAC readings for persons arrested for drunk driving, the *Birchfield* Court acknowledged the government's "paramount interest" in preserving public safety on highways, including the state's need to deter drunk driving from occurring in the first place through the imposition of criminal penalties for failing to cooperate with drunk driving investigations.[255] Weighing these competing interests, the Court ultimately concluded that the Fourth Amendment permits warrantless breath tests incident to arrests for drunk driving because the "impact of breath tests on privacy is slight," whereas the "need for BAC testing is great."[256] In so doing, the Court rejected the alternative of requiring the state to obtain a warrant prior to the administration of a BAC breath test, noting (1) the need for clear, categorical rules to provide police adequate guidance in the context of a search incident to an arrest and (2) the potential administrative burdens that would be incurred if warrants were required prior to every breathalyzer test.[257] Nonetheless, the Court reached a "different conclusion" with respect to *blood* tests, finding that such tests are "significantly more intrusive" and their "reasonability must be judged in light of the availability of the less intrusive alternative of a breath test."[258] As a consequence, the Court held that while a warrantless breath test

---

[251] *Id.*

[252] *Id.* at 20–22. The Court disclaimed a criminal defendant's possessory interest in the air in his lungs, as air in one's lungs is not a part of one's body and is regularly exhaled from the lungs as a natural process. *Id.* at 21.

[253] "Blood tests are a different matter." *Id.* at 22.

[254] *Id.* at 21–23.

[255] *Id.* at 24–25.

[256] *Id.* at 33.

[257] *Id.* at 25–28. The *Birchfield* Court also rejected "more costly" and previously tried alternatives to penalties for refusing a breath test, such as sobriety checkpoints, ignition interlocks, and the use of treatment programs. *Id.* at 29–30.

[258] *Id.* at 33. In so doing, the Court rejected the argument that warrantless blood tests are needed as an alternative to warrantless breath tests to detect impairing substances other than alcohol or to obtain the BAC of an unconscious or uncooperative driver. *Id.* at 34. In such situations, the Court reasoned that the state could

following a drunk-driving arrest is categorically permissible as a reasonable search under the Fourth Amendment, a warrantless blood test cannot be justified by the search incident to arrest doctrine.[259]

However, the Justices have long found themselves in disagreement about the scope of the search incident to arrest as it extends beyond the person to the area in which the person is arrested—most commonly either his premises or his vehicle. Certain early cases went both ways on the basis of some fine distinctions,[260] but in *Harris v. United States*,[261] the Court approved a search of a four-room apartment pursuant to an arrest under warrant for one crime, where the search turned up evidence of another crime. A year later, in *Trupiano v. United States*,[262] a raid on a distillery resulted in the arrest of a man found on the premises and a seizure of the equipment; the Court reversed the conviction because the officers had had time to obtain a search warrant and had not done so. "A search or seizure without a warrant as an incident to a lawful arrest has always been considered to be a strictly limited right. It grows out of the inherent necessities of the situation at the time of the arrest. But there must be something more in the way of necessity than merely a lawful arrest."[263]

The Court overruled *Trupiano* in *United States v. Rabinowitz*,[264] in which officers had arrested the defendant in his one-room office pursuant to an arrest warrant and proceeded to search the room completely. The Court observed that the issue was not whether the officers had the time and opportunity to obtain a search warrant but whether the search incident to arrest was reasonable. Though *Rabinowitz* referred to searches of the area within the arrestee's "immediate control,"[265] it provided no standard by which this area was to be determined, and extensive searches were permitted under the rule.[266]

---

obtain a warrant for the blood test, or in the case of an uncooperative driver, prosecute the defendant for refusing to undergo the breath test. *Id.* at 34–35.

[259] *Id.* at 37–38.

[260] *Compare* Marron v. United States, 275 U.S. 192 (1927), *with* Go-Bart Importing Co. v. United States, 282 U.S. 344 (1931), *and* United States v. Lefkowitz, 285 U.S. 452 (1932).

[261] 331 U.S. 145 (1947).

[262] 334 U.S. 699 (1948).

[263] 334 U.S. at 708.

[264] 339 U.S. 56 (1950).

[265] 339 U.S. at 64.

[266] *Cf.* Chimel v. California, 395 U.S. 752, 764–65 & n.10 (1969). But, in Kremen v. United States, 353 U.S. 346 (1957), the Court held that the seizure of the entire contents of a house and the removal to F.B.I. offices 200 miles away for examination, pursuant to an arrest under warrant of one of the persons found in the house, was unreasonable. In decisions contemporaneous to and subsequent to *Chimel*, applying pre-*Chimel* standards because that case was not retroactive, Williams v. United

In *Chimel v. California*,[267] however, a narrower view was asserted, the primacy of warrants was again emphasized, and a standard by which the scope of searches pursuant to arrest could be ascertained was set out. "When an arrest is made, it is reasonable for the arresting officer to search the person arrested in order to remove any weapons that the latter might seek to use in order to resist arrest or effect his escape. Otherwise, the officer's safety might well be endangered, and the arrest itself frustrated. In addition, it is entirely reasonable for the arresting officer to search for and seize any evidence on the arrestee's person in order to prevent its concealment or destruction. And the area into which an arrestee might reach in order to grab a weapon or evidentiary items must, of course, be governed by a like rule. A gun on a table or in a drawer in front of someone who is arrested can be as dangerous to the arresting officer as one concealed in the clothing of the person arrested. There is ample justification, therefore, for a search of the arrestee's person and the area 'within his immediate control'—construing that phrase to mean the area from within which he might gain possession of a weapon or destructible evidence."

"There is no comparable justification, however, for routinely searching any room other than that in which an arrest occurs—or, for that matter, for searching through all the desk drawers or other closed or concealed areas in that room itself. Such searches, in the absence of well-recognized exceptions, may be made only under the authority of a search warrant."[268]

Although the viability of *Chimel* had been in doubt for some time as the Court refined and applied its analysis of reasonable and justifiable expectations of privacy,[269] it has in some but not all contexts survived the changed rationale. Thus, in *Mincey v. Arizona*,[270] the Court rejected a state effort to create a "homicide-scene" exception for a warrantless search of an entire apartment extending over four days. The occupant had been arrested and removed and it was true, the Court observed, that a person legally

States, 401 U.S. 646 (1971), the Court has applied *Rabinowitz* somewhat restrictively. *See* Von Cleef v. New Jersey, 395 U.S. 814 (1969), which followed *Kremen*; Shipley v. California, 395 U.S. 818 (1969), and Vale v. Louisiana, 399 U.S. 30 (1970) (both involving arrests outside the house with subsequent searches of the house); Coolidge v. New Hampshire, 403 U.S. 443, 455–57 (1971). Substantially extensive searches were, however, approved in Williams v. United States, 401 U.S. 646 (1971), and Hill v. California, 401 U.S. 797 (1971).

[267] 395 U.S. 752 (1969).

[268] 395 U.S. at 762–63.

[269] *See, e.g.*, Coolidge v. New Hampshire, 403 U.S. 443, 492, 493, 510 (1971), in which the four dissenters advocated the reasonableness argument rejected in *Chimel*.

[270] 437 U.S. 385, 390–91 (1978). *Accord*, Flippo v. West Virginia, 528 U.S. 11 (1999) (per curiam).

taken into custody has a lessened right of privacy in his person, but he does not have a lessened right of privacy in his entire house. And, in *United States v. Chadwick*,[271] emphasizing a person's reasonable expectation of privacy in his luggage or other baggage, the Court held that, once police have arrested and immobilized a suspect, validly seized bags are not subject to search without a warrant.[272] Police may, however, in the course of jailing an arrested suspect, conduct an inventory search of the individual's personal effects, including the contents of a shoulder bag, since "the scope of a stationhouse search may in some circumstances be even greater than those supporting a search immediately following arrest."[273]

Chimel has, however, been qualified by another consideration. Not only may officers search areas within the arrestee's immediate control in order to alleviate any threat posed by the arrestee, but they may extend that search if there may be a threat posed by "unseen third parties in the house." A "protective sweep" of the entire premises (including an arrestee's home) may be undertaken on less than probable cause if officers have a "reasonable belief," based on "articulable facts," that the area to be swept may harbor an individual posing a danger to those on the arrest scene.[274]

Stating that it was "in no way alter[ing] the fundamental principles established in the *Chimel* case," the Court in *New York v. Belton*[275] held that police officers who had made a valid arrest of the occupant of a vehicle could make a contemporaneous search of the entire passenger compartment of the automobile, including containers found therein. Believing that a fairly simple rule understandable to authorities in the field was desirable, the Court ruled "that articles inside the relatively narrow compass of the passenger compartment of an automobile are in fact generally, if not inevitably,

---

[271] 433 U.S. 1 (1977). Defendant and his luggage, a footlocker, had been removed to the police station, where the search took place.

[272] If, on the other hand, a sealed shipping container had already been opened and resealed during a valid customs inspection, and officers had maintained surveillance through a "controlled delivery" to the suspect, there is no reasonable expectation of privacy in the contents of the container and officers may search it, upon the arrest of the suspect, without having obtained a warrant. Illinois v. Andreas, 463 U.S. 765 (1983).

[273] Illinois v. LaFayette, 462 U.S. 640, 645 (1983) (inventory search) (following South Dakota v. Opperman, 428 U.S. 364 (1976)). Similarly, an inventory search of an impounded vehicle may include the contents of a closed container. Colorado v. Bertine, 479 U.S. 367 (1987). Inventory searches of closed containers must, however, be guided by a police policy containing standardized criteria for exercise of discretion. Florida v. Wells, 495 U.S. 1 (1990).

[274] Maryland v. Buie, 494 U.S. 325, 334 (1990). This "sweep" is not to be a full-blown, "top-to-bottom" search, but only "a cursory inspection of those spaces where a person may be found." Id. at 335–36.

[275] 453 U.S. 454, 460 n.3 (1981).

within 'the area into which an arrestee might reach in order to grab a weapon or evidentiary ite[m].'"[276]

Belton was "widely understood to allow a vehicle search incident to the arrest of a recent occupant even if there is no possibility the arrestee could gain access to the vehicle at the time of the search."[277] In *Arizona v. Gant,*[278] however, the Court disavowed this understanding of *Belton*[279] and held that "[p]olice may search a vehicle incident to a recent occupant's arrest only if the arrestee is within reaching distance of the passenger compartment at the time of the search or it is reasonable to believe that the vehicle contains evidence of the offense of arrest."[280]

Vehicular Searches.—In the early days of the automobile, the Court created an exception for searches of vehicles, holding in *Carroll v. United States*[281] that vehicles may be searched without warrants if the officer undertaking the search has probable cause to believe that the vehicle contains contraband. The Court explained that the mobility of vehicles would allow them to be quickly moved from the jurisdiction if time were taken to obtain a warrant.[282]

Initially, the Court limited *Carroll's* reach, holding impermissible the warrantless seizure of a parked automobile merely because it is movable, and indicating that vehicles may be stopped only while moving or reasonably contemporaneously with move-

---

[276] 453 U.S. at 460 (quoting Chimel v. California, 395 U.S. 752, 763 (1969)). In this particular instance, Belton had been removed from the automobile and handcuffed, but the Court wished to create a general rule removed from the fact-specific nature of any one case. "'Container' here denotes any object capable of holding another object. It thus includes closed or open glove compartments, consoles, or other receptacles located anywhere within the passenger compartment, as well as luggage, boxes, bags, clothing, and the like. Our holding encompasses only the interior of the passenger compartment of an automobile and does not encompass the trunk." 453 U.S. at 460–61 n.4.

[277] Arizona v. Gant, 556 U.S. ___, No. 07–542, slip op. at 8 (2009).

[278] 556 U.S. ___, No. 07–542 (2009).

[279] "To read *Belton* as authorizing a vehicle search incident to every recent occupant's arrest would . . . untether the rule from the justifications underlying the *Chimel* exception . . . ." Slip op. at 9.

[280] 556 U.S. ___, No. 07–542, slip op. at 18. Justice Alito, in a dissenting opinion joined by Chief Justice Roberts and Justice Kennedy and in part by Justice Breyer, wrote that "there can be no doubt that" the majority had overruled *Belton*. Slip op. at 2.

[281] 267 U.S. 132 (1925). *Carroll* was a Prohibition-era liquor case, whereas a great number of modern automobile cases involve drugs.

[282] 267 U.S. at 153. *See also* Husty v. United States, 282 U.S. 694 (1931); Scher v. United States, 305 U.S. 251 (1938); Brinegar v. United States, 338 U.S. 160 (1949). All of these cases involved contraband, but in Chambers v. Maroney, 399 U.S. 42 (1970), the Court, without discussion, and over Justice Harlan's dissent, id. at 55, 62, extended the rule to evidentiary searches.

ment.[283] The Court also ruled that the search must be reasonably contemporaneous with the stop, so that it was not permissible to remove the vehicle to the station house for a warrantless search at the convenience of the police.[284]

The Court next developed a reduced privacy rationale to supplement the mobility rationale, explaining that "the configuration, use, and regulation of automobiles often may dilute the reasonable expectation of privacy that exists with respect to differently situated property."[285] "One has a lesser expectation of privacy in a motor vehicle because its function is transportation and it seldom serves as one's residence or as the repository of personal effects. . . . It travels public thoroughfares where both its occupants and its contents are in plain view.'"[286] Although motor homes serve as residences and as repositories for personal effects, and their contents are often shielded from public view, the Court extended the automobile exception to them as well, holding that there is a diminished expectation of privacy in a mobile home parked in a parking lot and licensed for vehicular travel, hence "readily mobile."[287]

The reduced expectancy concept has broadened police powers to conduct automobile searches without warrants, but they still must have probable cause to search a vehicle[288] and they may not make random stops of vehicles on the roads, but instead must base stops of individual vehicles on probable cause or some "articulable and reasonable suspicion"[289] of traffic or safety violation or some other

---

[283] Coolidge v. New Hampshire, 403 U.S. 443, 458–64 (1971). This portion of the opinion had the adherence of a plurality only, Justice Harlan concurring on other grounds, and there being four dissenters. Id. at 493, 504, 510, 523.

[284] Preston v. United States, 376 U.S. 364 (1964); Dyke v. Taylor Implement Mfg. Co., 391 U.S. 216 (1968).

[285] Arkansas v. Sanders, 442 U.S. 753, 761 (1979).

[286] Cardwell v. Lewis, 417 U.S. 583, 590 (1974) (plurality opinion), *quoted in* United States v. Chadwick, 433 U.S. 1, 12 (1977). *See also* United States v. Ortiz, 422 U.S. 891, 896 (1975); United States v. Martinez-Fuerte, 428 U.S. 543, 561 (1976); South Dakota v. Opperman, 428 U.S. 364, 367–68 (1976); Robbins v. California, 453 U.S. 420, 424–25 (1981); United States v. Ross, 456 U.S. 798, 807 n.9 (1982).

[287] California v. Carney, 471 U.S. 386, 393 (1985) (leaving open the question of whether the automobile exception also applies to a "mobile" home being used as a residence and not "readily mobile").

[288] Almeida-Sanchez v. United States, 413 U.S. 266 (1973) (roving patrols); United States v. Ortiz, 422 U.S. 891 (1975). *Cf.* Colorado v. Bannister, 449 U.S. 1 (1980). An automobile's "ready mobility [is] an exigency sufficient to excuse failure to obtain a search warrant once probable cause is clear"; there is no need to find the presence of "unforeseen circumstances" or other additional exigency. Pennsylvania v. Labron, 527 U.S. 465 (1996). *Accord,* Maryland v. Dyson, 527 U.S. 465 (1999) (per curiam). *Cf.* Florida v. Harris, 568 U.S. ___, No. 11–817, slip op. (2013).

[289] Delaware v. Prouse, 440 U.S. 648, 663 (1979) (discretionary random stops of motorists to check driver's license and automobile registration constitute Fourth Amendment violation); United States v. Brignoni-Ponce, 422 U.S. 873 (1975) (violation for roving patrols on lookout for illegal aliens to stop vehicles on highways near inter-

criminal activity.[290] If police stop a vehicle, then the vehicle's passengers as well as its driver are deemed to have been seized from the moment the car comes to a halt, and the passengers as well as the driver may challenge the constitutionality of the stop.[291] Likewise, a police officer may frisk (patdown for weapons) both the driver and any passengers whom he reasonably concludes "might be armed and presently dangerous."[292]

By contrast, fixed-checkpoint stops in the absence of any individualized suspicion have been upheld for purposes of promoting highway safety[293] or policing the international border,[294] but not for more generalized law enforcement purposes.[295] Once police have validly stopped a vehicle, they may also, based on articulable facts warranting a reasonable belief that weapons may be present, conduct a *Terry*-type protective search of those portions of the passenger compartment in which a weapon could be placed or hidden.[296] And, in the absence of such reasonable suspicion as to weapons,

national borders when only ground for suspicion is that occupants appear to be of Mexican ancestry). *But cf.* United States v. Arvizu, 534 U.S. 266 (2002) (reasonable suspicion justified stop by border agents of vehicle traveling on unpaved backroads in an apparent effort to evade a border patrol checkpoint on the highway). In *Prouse*, the Court cautioned that it was not precluding the states from developing methods for spot checks, such as questioning all traffic at roadblocks, that involve less intrusion or that do not involve unconstrained exercise of discretion. 440 U.S. at 663.

[290] An officer who observes a traffic violation may stop a vehicle even if his real motivation is to investigate for evidence of other crime. Whren v. United States, 517 U.S. 806 (1996). The existence of probable cause to believe that a traffic violation has occurred establishes the constitutional reasonableness of traffic stops regardless of the actual motivation of the officers involved, and regardless of whether it is customary police practice to stop motorists for the violation observed. Similarly, pretextual arrest of a motorist who has committed a traffic offense is permissible. Arkansas v. Sullivan, 532 U.S. 769 (2001) (per curiam) (upholding search of the motorist's car for a crime not related to the traffic offense).

[291] Brendlin v. California, 551 U.S. 249, 263 (2007).

[292] Arizona v. Johnson, 129 S. Ct. 781, 786 (2009).

[293] Michigan Dep't of State Police v. Sitz, 496 U.S. 444 (1990) (upholding a sobriety checkpoint at which all motorists are briefly stopped for preliminary questioning and observation for signs of intoxication).

[294] United States v. Martinez-Fuerte, 428 U.S. 543 (1976) (upholding border patrol checkpoint, over 60 miles from the border, for questioning designed to apprehend illegal aliens). *See also* United States v. Flores-Montano, 541 U.S. 149 (2004) (upholding a search at the border involving disassembly of a vehicle's fuel tank).

[295] City of Indianapolis v. Edmond, 531 U.S. 32 (2000) (vehicle checkpoint set up for the "primary purpose [of] detect[ing] evidence of ordinary criminal wrongdoing" (here interdicting illegal narcotics) does not fall within the highway safety or border patrol exception to the individualized suspicion requirement, and hence violates the Fourth Amendment). *Edmond* was distinguished in Illinois v. Lidster, 540 U.S. 419 (2004), upholding use of a checkpoint to ask motorists for help in solving a recent hit-and-run accident that had resulted in death. The public interest in solving the crime was deemed "grave," while the interference with personal liberty was deemed minimal.

[296] Michigan v. Long, 463 U.S. 1032, 1049 (1983) (holding that contraband found in the course of such a search is admissible).

police may seize contraband and suspicious items "in plain view" inside the passenger compartment.[297]

Although officers who have stopped a car to issue a routine traffic citation may conduct a *Terry*-type search, even including a patdown of driver and passengers if there is reasonable suspicion that they are armed and dangerous, they may not conduct a full-blown search of the car[298] unless they exercise their discretion to arrest the driver instead of issuing a citation.[299] And once police have probable cause to believe there is contraband in a vehicle, they may remove the vehicle from the scene to the station house in order to conduct a search, without thereby being required to obtain a warrant.[300] "[T]he justification to conduct such a warrantless search does not vanish once the car has been immobilized; nor does it depend upon a reviewing court's assessment of the likelihood in each particular case that the car would have been driven away, or that its contents would have been tampered with, during the period re-

---

[297] Texas v. Brown, 460 U.S. 730 (1983). Similarly, because there is no reasonable privacy interest in the vehicle identification number, required by law to be placed on the dashboard so as to be visible through the windshield, police may reach into the passenger compartment to remove items obscuring the number and may seize items in plain view while doing so. New York v. Class, 475 U.S. 106 (1986). Because there also is no legitimate privacy interest in possessing contraband, and because properly conducted canine sniffs are "generally likely[] to reveal only the presence of contraband," police may conduct a canine sniff around the perimeter of a vehicle stopped for a traffic offense so long as the stop is not prolonged beyond the time needed to process the traffic violation. *Compare* Illinois v. Caballes, 543 U.S. 405 (2005) (a canine sniff around the perimeter of a car following a routine traffic stop does not offend the Fourth Amendment if the duration of the stop is justified by the traffic offense) *with* Rodriguez v. United States, 575 U.S. ___, No. 13–9972, slip op. at 3, 5–6 (2015) (finding that the stop in question had been prolonged for seven to eight minutes beyond the time needed to resolve the traffic offense in order to conduct a canine sniff).

[298] Knowles v. Iowa, 525 U.S. 113 (1998) (invalidating an Iowa statute permitting a full-blown search incident to a traffic citation).

[299] *See* Atwater v. City of Lago Vista, 532 U.S. 318 (2001) (police officers, in their discretion, may arrest a motorist for a minor traffic offense rather than issuing a citation); New York v. Belton, 453 U.S. 454 (1981) (officers who arrest an occupant of a vehicle may make a contemporaneous search of the entire passenger compartment, including closed containers); Thornton v. United States, 541 U.S. 615 (2004) (the *Belton* rule applies regardless of whether the arrestee exited the car at the officer's direction, or whether he did so prior to confrontation); Arizona v. Gant, 556 U.S. ___, No. 07–542 (U.S. Apr. 21 (2009), slip op. at 18 (the *Belton* rule applies "only if the arrestee is within reaching distance of the passenger compartment at the time of the search or it is reasonable to believe that the vehicle contains evidence of the offense of arrest"); Arkansas v. Sullivan, 532 U.S. 769 (2001) (pretextual arrest of motorist who has committed a traffic offense is permissible even if purpose is to search vehicle for evidence of other crime).

[300] Michigan v. Thomas, 458 U.S. 259 (1982). The same rule applies if it is the vehicle itself that is forfeitable contraband; police, acting without a warrant, may seize the vehicle from a public place. Florida v. White, 526 U.S. 559 (1999).

quired for the police to obtain a warrant." [301] Because of the lessened expectation of privacy, inventory searches of impounded automobiles are justifiable in order to protect public safety and the owner's
property, and any evidence of criminal activity discovered in the course
of the inventories is admissible in court.[302] The Justices were evenly
divided, however, on the propriety of warrantless seizure of an arrestee's automobile from a public parking lot several hours after his
arrest, its transportation to a police impoundment lot, and the taking of tire casts and exterior paint scrapings.[303]

Police in undertaking a warrantless search of an automobile may
not extend the search to the persons of the passengers therein [304]
unless there is a reasonable suspicion that the passengers are armed
and dangerous, in which case a *Terry* patdown is permissible,[305] or
unless there is individualized suspicion of criminal activity by the
passengers.[306] But because passengers in an automobile have no reasonable expectation of privacy in the interior area of the car, a warrantless search of the glove compartment and the spaces under the
seats, which turned up evidence implicating the passengers, invaded no Fourth Amendment interest of the passengers.[307] Luggage and other closed containers found in automobiles may also be
subjected to warrantless searches based on probable cause, regardless of whether the luggage or containers belong to the driver or to
a passenger, and regardless of whether it is the driver or a passenger who is under suspicion.[308] The same rule now applies whether
the police have probable cause to search only the containers [309] or

---

[301] Michigan v. Thomas, 458 U.S. at 261. *See also* Chambers v. Maroney, 399
U.S. 42 (1970); Texas v. White, 423 U.S. 67 (1975); United States v. Ross, 456 U.S.
798, 807 n.9 (1982).

[302] Cady v. Dombrowski, 413 U.S. 433 (1973); South Dakota v. Opperman, 428
U.S. 364 (1976). *See also* Cooper v. California, 386 U.S. 58 (1967); United States v.
Harris, 390 U.S. 234 (1968). Police, in conducting an inventory search of a vehicle,
may open closed containers in order to inventory contents. Colorado v. Bertine, 479
U.S. 367 (1987).

[303] Cardwell v. Lewis, 417 U.S. 583 (1974). Justice Powell concurred on other
grounds.

[304] United States v. Di Re, 332 U.S. 581 (1948); Ybarra v. Illinois, 444 U.S. 85,
94–96 (1979).

[305] Knowles v. Iowa, 525 U.S. 113, 118 (1998).

[306] Maryland v. Pringle, 540 U.S. 366 (2003) (probable cause to arrest passengers based on officers finding $783 in glove compartment and cocaine hidden be-
neath back seat armrest, and on driver and passengers all denying ownership of
the cocaine).

[307] Rakas v. Illinois, 439 U.S. 128 (1978).

[308] Wyoming v. Houghton, 526 U.S. 295, 307 (1999) ("police officers with probable cause to search a car may inspect passengers' belongings found in the car that
are capable of concealing the object of the search").

[309] California v. Acevedo, 500 U.S. 565 (1991) (overruling Arkansas v. Sanders,
442 U.S. 753 (1979).

whether they have probable cause to search the automobile for something capable of being held in the container.[310]

Vessel Searches.—Not only is the warrant requirement inapplicable to brief stops of vessels, but also none of the safeguards applicable to stops of automobiles on less than probable cause are necessary predicates to stops of vessels. In *United States v. Villamonte-Marquez*,[311] the Court upheld a random stop and boarding of a vessel by customs agents, lacking any suspicion of wrongdoing, for purpose of inspecting documentation. The boarding was authorized by statute derived from an act of the First Congress,[312] and hence had "an impressive historical pedigree" carrying with it a presumption of constitutionality. Moreover, "important factual differences between vessels located in waters offering ready access to the open sea and automobiles on principal thoroughfares in the border area" justify application of a less restrictive rule for vessel searches. The reason why random stops of vehicles have been held impermissible under the Fourth Amendment, the Court explained, is that stops at fixed checkpoints or roadblocks are both feasible and less subject to abuse of discretion by authorities. "But no reasonable claim can be made that permanent checkpoints would be practical on waters such as these where vessels can move in any direction at any time and need not follow established 'avenues' as automobiles must do."[313] Because there is a "substantial" governmental interest in enforcing documentation laws, "especially in waters where the need to deter or apprehend smugglers is great," the Court found the "limited" but not "minimal" intrusion occasioned by boarding for documentation inspection to be reasonable.[314] Dissenting Justice Brennan argued that the Court for the first time was approving "a completely random seizure and detention of persons and an entry onto private, noncommercial premises by police officers, without any

---

[310] United States v. Ross, 456 U.S. 798 (1982). A *Ross* search of a container found in an automobile need not occur soon after its seizure. United States v. Johns, 469 U.S. 478 (1985) (three-day time lapse). *See also* Florida v. Jimeno, 500 U.S. 248 (1991) (consent to search automobile for drugs constitutes consent to open containers within the car that might contain drugs).

[311] 462 U.S. 579 (1983).

[312] 19 U.S.C. § 1581(a), derived from § 31 of the Act of Aug. 4, 1790, ch. 35, 1 Stat. 164.

[313] 462 U.S. at 589. Justice Brennan's dissent argued that a fixed checkpoint was feasible in this case, involving a ship channel in an inland waterway. Id. at 608 n.10. The fact that the Court's rationale was geared to the difficulties of law enforcement in the open seas suggests a reluctance to make exceptions to the general rule. Note as well the Court's later reference to this case as among those "reflect[ing] longstanding concern for the protection of the integrity of the border." United States v. Montoya de Hernandez, 473 U.S. 531, 538 (1985).

[314] 462 U.S. at 593.

limitations whatever on the officers' discretion or any safeguards against abuse." [315]

Consent Searches.—Fourth Amendment rights, like other constitutional rights, may be waived, and one may consent to a search of his person or premises by officers who have not complied with the Amendment. [316] The Court, however, has insisted that the burden is on the prosecution to prove the voluntariness of the consent [317] and awareness of the right of choice. [318] Reviewing courts must determine on the basis of the totality of the circumstances whether consent has been freely given or has been coerced. Actual knowledge of the right to refuse consent is not essential for a search to be found voluntary, and police therefore are not required to inform a person of his rights, as through a Fourth Amendment version of *Miranda* warnings. [319] But consent will not be regarded as voluntary when the officer asserts his official status and claim of right and the occupant yields because of these factors. [320] When consent is obtained through the deception of an undercover officer or an informer's gaining admission without advising a suspect who he is, the Court has held that the suspect has simply assumed the risk that an invitee would betray him, and evidence obtained through the deception is admissible. [321] Moreover, while the Court has appeared to endorse implied consent laws that view individuals who engage in certain regulated activities as having implicitly agreed

---

[315] 462 U.S. at 598. Justice Brennan contended that all previous cases had required some "discretion-limiting" feature such as a requirement of probable cause, reasonable suspicion, fixed checkpoints instead of roving patrols, and limitation of border searches to border areas, and that these principles set forth in Delaware v. Prouse, 440 U.S. 648 (1979), should govern. Id. at 599, 601.

[316] Amos v. United States, 255 U.S. 313 (1921); Zap v. United States, 328 U.S. 624 (1946); Schneckloth v. Bustamonte, 412 U.S. 218 (1973).

[317] Bumper v. North Carolina, 391 U.S. 543 (1968).

[318] Johnson v. United States, 333 U.S. 10, 13 (1948).

[319] Schneckloth v. Bustamonte, 412 U.S. 218, 231–33 (1973). See also Ohio v. Robinette, 519 U.S. 33 (1996) (officer need not always inform a detained motorist that he is free to go before consent to search auto may be deemed voluntary); United States v. Drayton, 536 U.S. 194, 207 (2002) (totality of circumstances indicated that bus passenger consented to search even though officer did not explicitly state that passenger was free to refuse permission).

[320] Amos v. United States, 255 U.S. 313 (1921); Johnson v. United States, 333 U.S. 10 (1948); Bumper v. North Carolina, 391 U.S. 543 (1968).

[321] On Lee v. United States, 343 U.S. 747 (1952); Lopez v. United States, 373 U.S. 427 (1963); Hoffa v. United States, 385 U.S. 293 (1966); Lewis v. United States, 385 U.S. 206 (1966); United States v. White, 401 U.S. 745 (1971). *Cf.* Osborn v. United States, 385 U.S. 323 (1966) (prior judicial approval obtained before wired informer sent into defendant's presence). Problems may be encountered by police, however, in special circumstances. *See* Massiah v. United States, 377 U.S. 201 (1964); United States v. Henry, 447 U.S. 264 (1980); United States v. Karo, 468 U.S. 705 (1984) (installation of beeper with consent of informer who sold container with beeper to suspect is permissible with prior judicial approval, but use of beeper to monitor private residence is not).

to certain searches related to that activity and the enforcement of such laws through civil penalties,[322] the implied consent doctrine does not extend so far as to deem individuals to have impliedly consented to a search on "pain of committing a criminal offense."[323]

Additional issues arise in determining the validity of consent to search when consent is given not by the suspect, but by a third party. In the earlier cases, third-party consent was deemed sufficient if that party "possessed common authority over or other sufficient relationship to the premises or effects sought to be inspected."[324] Now, however, actual common authority over the premises is not required; it is sufficient if the searching officer had a reasonable but mistaken belief that the third party had common authority and could consent to the search.[325] If, however, one occupant consents to a search of shared premises, but a physically present co-occupant expressly objects to the search, the search is unreasonable.[326] Common social expectations inform the analysis. A person at the threshold of a residence could not confidently conclude he was welcome to enter over the express objection of a present cotenant. Expectations may change, however, if the objecting co-

---

[322] *See, e.g.*, Missouri v. McNeely, 569 U.S. ___, No. 11–1425, slip op. at 18 (2013) (plurality opinion) (discussing implied consent laws that "require motorists, as a condition of operating a motor vehicle, . . . to consent to [blood alcohol concentration] testing if they are arrested or otherwise detained on suspicion of a drunk-driving offense" or risk losing their license); South Dakota v. Neville, 459 U.S. 553, 554, 563–64 (1983).

[323] See Birchfield v. North Dakota, 579 U.S. ___, No. 14–1468, slip op. at 36–37 (2016).

[324] United States v. Matlock, 415 U.S. 164, 171 (1974) (valid consent by woman with whom defendant was living and sharing the bedroom searched). *See also* Chapman v. United States, 365 U.S. 610 (1961) (landlord's consent insufficient); Stoner v. California, 376 U.S. 483 (1964) (hotel desk clerk lacked authority to consent to search of guest's room); Frazier v. Culp, 394 U.S. 731 (1969) (joint user of duffel bag had authority to consent to search).

[325] Illinois v. Rodriguez, 497 U.S. 177 (1990). *See also* Florida v. Jimeno, 500 U.S. 248, 251 (1991) (it was "objectively reasonable" for officer to believe that suspect's consent to search his car for narcotics included consent to search containers found within the car).

[326] Georgia v. Randolph, 547 U.S. 103 (2006) (warrantless search of a defendant's residence based on his estranged wife's consent was unreasonable and invalid as applied to a physically present defendant who expressly refused to permit entry). The Court in *Randolph* admitted that it was "drawing a fine line," id. at 121, between situations where the defendant is present and expressly refuses consent, and that of United States v. Matlock, 415 U.S. 164, 171 (1974), and Illinois v. Rodriguez, 497 U.S. 177 (1990), where the defendants were nearby but were not asked for their permission. In a dissenting opinion, Chief Justice Roberts observed that the majority's ruling "provides protection on a random and happenstance basis, protecting, for example, a co-occupant who happens to be at the front door when the other occupant consents to a search, but not one napping or watching television in the next room." 547 U.S. at 127.

tenant leaves, or is removed from, the premises with no prospect of imminent return.[327]

Border Searches.—"That searches made at the border, pursuant to the longstanding right of the sovereign to protect itself by stopping and examining persons and property crossing into this country, are reasonable simply by virtue of the fact that they occur at the border, should, by now, require no extended demonstration."[328] Authorized by the First Congress,[329] the customs search in these circumstances requires no warrant, no probable cause, not even the showing of some degree of suspicion that accompanies even investigatory stops.[330] Moreover, although prolonged detention of travelers beyond the routine customs search and inspection must be justified by the *Terry* standard of reasonable suspicion having a particularized and objective basis, *Terry* protections as to the length and intrusiveness of the search do not apply.[331] Motor vehicles may be searched at the border, even to the extent of removing, disassembling, and reassembling the fuel tank.[332]

Inland stoppings and searches in areas away from the borders are a different matter altogether. Thus, in *Almeida-Sanchez v. United States*,[333] the Court held that a warrantless stop and search of defendant's automobile on a highway some 20 miles from the border

---

[327] Fernandez v. California, 571 U.S. ___, No. 12–7822, slip op. (2014) (consent by co-occupant sufficient to overcome objection of a second co-occupant who was arrested and removed from the premises, so long as the arrest and removal were objectively reasonable).

[328] United States v. Ramsey, 431 U.S. 606, 616 (1977) (sustaining search of incoming mail). *See also* Illinois v. Andreas, 463 U.S. 765 (1983) (opening by customs inspector of locked container shipped from abroad).

[329] Act of July 31, 1789, ch. 5, §§ 23, 24, 1 Stat. 43. *See* 19 U.S.C. §§ 507, 1581, 1582.

[330] Carroll v. United States, 267 U.S. 132, 154 (1925); United States v. Thirty-seven Photographs, 402 U.S. 363, 376 (1971); Almeida-Sanchez v. United States, 413 U.S. 266, 272 (1973).

[331] United States v. Montoya de Hernandez, 473 U.S. 531 (1985) (approving warrantless detention incommunicado for more than 24 hours of traveler suspected of alimentary canal drug smuggling). The traveler was strip searched, and then given a choice between an abdominal x-ray or monitored bowel movements. Because the suspect chose the latter option, the court disavowed decision as to "what level of suspicion, if any, is required for . . . strip, body cavity, or involuntary x-ray searches." Id. at 541 n.4.

[332] United States v. Flores-Montano, 541 U.S. 149 (2004).

[333] 413 U.S. 266 (1973). Justices White, Blackmun, Rehnquist, and Chief Justice Burger would have found the search reasonable upon the congressional determination that searches by such roving patrols were the only effective means to police border smuggling. Id. at 285. Justice Powell, concurring, argued in favor of a general, administrative warrant authority not tied to particular vehicles, much like the type of warrant suggested for noncriminal administrative inspections of homes and commercial establishments for health and safety purposes, id. at 275, but the Court has not yet had occasion to pass on a specific case. *See* United States v. Martinez-Fuerte, 428 U.S. 543, 547 n.2, 562 n.15 (1976).

by a roving patrol lacking probable cause to believe that the vehicle contained illegal aliens violated the Fourth Amendment. Similarly, the Court invalidated an automobile search at a fixed checkpoint well removed from the border; while agreeing that a fixed checkpoint probably gave motorists less cause for alarm than did roving patrols, the Court nonetheless held that the invasion of privacy entailed in a search was just as intrusive and must be justified by a showing of probable cause or consent.[334] On the other hand, when motorists are briefly stopped, not for purposes of a search but in order that officers may inquire into their residence status, either by asking a few questions or by checking papers, different results are achieved, so long as the stops are not truly random. Roving patrols may stop vehicles for purposes of a brief inquiry, provided officers are "aware of specific articulable facts, together with rational inferences from those facts, that reasonably warrant suspicion" that an automobile contains illegal aliens; in such a case the interference with Fourth Amendment rights is "modest" and the law enforcement interests served are significant.[335] Fixed checkpoints provide additional safeguards; here officers may halt all vehicles briefly in order to question occupants even in the absence of any reasonable suspicion that the particular vehicle contains illegal aliens.[336]

"Open Fields".—In *Hester v. United States*,[337] the Court held that the Fourth Amendment did not protect "open fields" and that, therefore, police searches in such areas as pastures, wooded areas, open water, and vacant lots need not comply with the requirements of warrants and probable cause. The Court's announcement in *Katz v. United States*[338] that the Amendment protects "people not places" cast some doubt on the vitality of the open fields prin-

---

[334] United States v. Ortiz, 422 U.S. 891 (1975).

[335] United States v. Brignoni-Ponce, 422 U.S. 873 (1975). However, stopping of defendant's car solely because the officers observed the Mexican appearance of the occupants was unjustified. Id. at 886. *Contrast* United States v. Cortez, 449 U.S. 411 (1981), and United States v. Arvizu, 534 U.S. 266 (2002), where border agents did have grounds for reasonable suspicion that the vehicle they stopped contained illegal aliens.

[336] United States v. Martinez-Fuerte, 428 U.S. 543 (1976). The Court deemed the intrusion on Fourth Amendment interests to be quite limited, even if officers acted on the basis of the Mexican appearance of the occupants in referring motorists to a secondary inspection area for questioning, whereas the elimination of the practice would deny to the government its only practicable way to apprehend smuggled aliens and to deter the practice. Similarly, outside of the border/aliens context, the Court has upheld use of fixed "sobriety" checkpoints at which all motorists are briefly stopped for preliminary questioning and observation for signs of intoxication. Michigan Dep't of State Police v. Sitz, 496 U.S. 444 (1990).

[337] 265 U.S. 57 (1924). *See also* Air Pollution Variance Bd. v. Western Alfalfa Corp., 416 U.S. 86 (1974).

[338] 389 U.S. 347, 353 (1967). *Cf.* Cady v. Dombrowski, 413 U.S. 433, 450 (1973) (citing *Hester* approvingly).

ciple, but all such doubts were cast away in *Oliver v. United States*.[339] Invoking *Hester's* reliance on the literal wording of the Fourth Amendment (open fields are not "effects") and distinguishing *Katz*, the Court ruled that the open fields exception applies to fields that are fenced and posted. "[A]n individual may not legitimately demand privacy for activities conducted out of doors in fields, except in the area immediately surrounding the home."[340] Nor may an individual demand privacy for activities conducted within outbuildings and visible by trespassers peering into the buildings from just outside.[341] Even within the curtilage and notwithstanding that the owner has gone to the extreme of erecting a 10-foot high fence in order to screen the area from ground-level view, there is no reasonable expectation of privacy from naked-eye inspection from fixed-wing aircraft flying in navigable airspace.[342] Similarly, naked-eye inspection from helicopters flying even lower contravenes no reasonable expectation of privacy.[343] And aerial photography of commercial facilities secured from ground-level public view is permissible, the Court finding such spaces more analogous to open fields than to the curtilage of a dwelling.[344]

"Plain View".—Somewhat similar in rationale is the rule that objects falling in the "plain view" of an officer who has a right to be in the position to have that view are subject to seizure without a warrant[345] or that, if the officer needs a warrant or probable cause to search and seize, his lawful observation will provide grounds there-

[339] 466 U.S. 170 (1984) (approving warrantless intrusion past no trespassing signs and around locked gate, to view field not visible from outside property).

[340] 466 U.S. at 178. *See also* California v. Greenwood, 486 U.S. 35 (1988) (approving warrantless search of garbage left curbside "readily accessible to animals, children, scavengers, snoops, and other members of the public").

[341] United States v. Dunn, 480 U.S. 294 (1987) (space immediately outside a barn, accessible only after crossing a series of "ranch-style" fences and situated one-half mile from the public road, constitutes unprotected "open field").

[342] California v. Ciraolo, 476 U.S. 207 (1986). Activities within the curtilage are nonetheless still entitled to some Fourth Amendment protection. The Court has described four considerations for determining whether an area falls within the curtilage: proximity to the home, whether the area is included within an enclosure also surrounding the home, the nature of the uses to which the area is put, and the steps taken by the resident to shield the area from view of passersby. United States v. Dunn, 480 U.S. 294 (1987) (barn 50 yards outside of fence surrounding home, used for processing chemicals, and separated from public access only by a series of livestock fences, by a chained and locked driveway, and by one-half mile's distance, is not within curtilage).

[343] Florida v. Riley, 488 U.S. 445 (1989) (view through partially open roof of greenhouse).

[344] Dow Chemical Co. v. United States, 476 U.S. 227 (1986) (suggesting that aerial photography of the curtilage would be impermissible).

[345] Washington v. Chrisman, 455 U.S. 1 (1982) (officer lawfully in dorm room may seize marijuana seeds and pipe in open view); United States v. Santana, 427 U.S. 38 (1976) ("plain view" justification for officers to enter home to arrest after observing defendant standing in open doorway); Harris v. United States, 390 U.S.

for.[346] The plain view doctrine is limited, however, by the probable cause requirement: officers must have probable cause to believe that items in plain view are contraband before they may search or seize them.[347]

The Court has analogized from the plain view doctrine to hold that, once officers have lawfully observed contraband, "the owner's privacy interest in that item is lost," and officers may reseal a container, trace its path through a controlled delivery, and seize and reopen the container without a warrant.[348]

Public Schools.—In *New Jersey v. T.L.O.*,[349] the Court set forth the principles governing searches by public school authorities. The Fourth Amendment applies to searches conducted by public school officials because "school officials act as representatives of the State, not merely as surrogates for the parents."[350] However, "the school setting requires some easing of the restrictions to which searches by public authorities are ordinarily subject."[351] Neither the warrant requirement nor the probable cause standard is appropriate, the Court ruled. Instead, a simple reasonableness standard governs all searches of students' persons and effects by school authorities.[352] A search must be reasonable at its inception, *i.e.*, there must

234 (1968) (officer who opened door of impounded automobile and saw evidence in plain view properly seized it); Ker v. California, 374 U.S. 23 (1963) (officers entered premises without warrant to make arrest because of exigent circumstances seized evidence in plain sight). *Cf.* Coolidge v. New Hampshire, 403 U.S. 443, 464–73 (1971), and id. at 510 (Justice White dissenting). Maryland v. Buie, 494 U.S. 325 (1990) (items seized in plain view during protective sweep of home incident to arrest); Texas v. Brown, 460 U.S. 730 (1983) (contraband on car seat in plain view of officer who had stopped car and asked for driver's license); New York v. Class, 475 U.S. 106 (1986) (evidence seen while looking for vehicle identification number). There is no requirement that the discovery of evidence in plain view must be "inadvertent." *See* Horton v. California, 496 U.S. 128 (1990) (in spite of Amendment's particularity requirement, officers with warrant to search for *proceeds* of robbery may seize *weapons* of robbery in plain view).

346 Steele v. United States, 267 U.S. 498 (1925) (officers observed contraband in view through open doorway; had probable cause to procure warrant). *Cf.* Taylor v. United States, 286 U.S. 1 (1932) (officers observed contraband in plain view in garage, warrantless entry to seize was unconstitutional).

347 Arizona v. Hicks, 480 U.S. 321 (1987) (police lawfully in apartment to investigate shooting lacked probable cause to inspect expensive stereo equipment to record serial numbers).

348 Illinois v. Andreas, 463 U.S. 765, 771 (1983) (locker customs agents had opened, and which was subsequently traced). *Accord*, United States v. Jacobsen, 466 U.S. 109 (1984) (inspection of package opened by private freight carrier who notified drug agents).

349 469 U.S. 325 (1985).

350 469 U.S. at 336.

351 469 U.S. at 340.

352 This single rule, the Court explained, will permit school authorities "to regulate their conduct according to the dictates of reason and common sense." 469 U.S. at 343. Rejecting the suggestion of dissenting Justice Stevens, the Court was "unwill-

be "reasonable grounds for suspecting that the search will turn up evidence that the student has violated or is violating either the law or the rules of the school." [353] School searches must also be reasonably related in scope to the circumstances justifying the interference, and "not excessively intrusive in light of the age and sex of the student and the nature of the infraction." [354] In applying these rules, the Court upheld as reasonable the search of a student's purse to determine whether the student, accused of violating a school rule by smoking in the lavatory, possessed cigarettes. The search for cigarettes uncovered evidence of drug activity held admissible in a prosecution under the juvenile laws.

In *Safford Unified School District #1 v. Redding*,[355] a student found in possession of prescription ibuprofen pills at school stated that the pills had come from another student, 13-year-old Savana Redding. The Court found that the first student's statement was sufficiently plausible to warrant suspicion that Savana was involved in pill distribution, and that this suspicion was enough to justify a search of Savana's backpack and outer clothing.[356] School officials, however, had also "directed Savana to remove her clothes down to her underwear, and then 'pull out' her bra and the elastic band on her underpants"[357]—an action that the Court thought could fairly be labeled a strip search. Taking into account that "adolescent vulnerability intensifies the patent intrusiveness of the exposure" and that, according to a study, a strip search can "result in serious emotional damage," the Court found that the search violated the Fourth Amendment.[358] "Because there were no reasons to suspect the drugs presented a danger or were concealed in her underwear," the Court wrote, "the content of the suspicion failed to match the degree of intrusion."[359] But, even though the Court found that the search had violated the Fourth Amendment, it found that the school officials who conducted the search were protected from

ing to adopt a standard under which the legality of a search is dependent upon a judge's evaluation of the relative importance of various school rules." Id. at n.9.

[353] 469 U.S. at 342. The Court has further elaborated that this "reasonable suspicion" standard is met if there is a "moderate chance" of finding evidence of wrongdoing. Safford Unified School District #1 v. Redding, 557 U.S. ___, No. 08–479, slip op. at 5 (2009).

[354] 469 U.S. at 342.

[355] 557 U.S. ___, No. 08–479 (2009).

[356] 557 U.S. ___, No. 08–479, slip op. at 7.

[357] 557 U.S. ___, No. 08–479, slip op. at 8.

[358] 557 U.S. ___, No. 08–479, slip op. at 8.

[359] 557 U.S. ___, No. 08–479, slip op. at 1, 9. Justice Thomas dissented from the finding of a Fourth Amendment violation.

liability through qualified immunity, because the law prior to *Redding* was not clearly established.[360]

Government Workplace.—Similar principles apply to a public employer's work-related search of its employees' offices, desks, or file cabinets, except that in this context the Court distinguished searches conducted for law enforcement purposes. In *O'Connor v. Ortega*,[361] a majority of Justices agreed, albeit on somewhat differing rationales, that neither a warrant nor a probable cause requirement should apply to employer searches "for noninvestigatory, work-related purposes, as well as for investigations of work-related misconduct."[362] Four Justices would require a case-by-case inquiry into the reasonableness of such searches;[363] one would hold that such searches "do not violate the Fourth Amendment."[364]

In *City of Ontario v. Quon*,[365] the Court bypassed adopting an approach for determining a government employee's reasonable expectation of privacy, an issue unresolved in *O'Connor*. Rather, the *Quon* Court followed the "special needs" holding in *O'Connor* and found that, even assuming a reasonable expectation of privacy, a city's warrantless search of the transcripts of a police officer's on-duty text messages on city equipment was reasonable because it was justified at its inception by noninvestigatory work-related purposes and was not excessively intrusive.[366] A jury had found the purpose of the search to be to determine whether the city's contract with its wireless service provider was adequate, and the Court held that "reviewing the transcripts was reasonable because it was an efficient and expedient way to determine whether [the officer's] overages were the result of work-related messaging or personal use."[367]

Prisons and Regulation of Probation and Parole.—The "undoubted security imperatives involved in jail supervision" require "defer[ence] to the judgment of correctional officials unless the record contains substantial evidence showing their policies are an unnecessary or unjustified response to the problems of jail secu-

---

[360] *See* "Alternatives to the Exclusionary Rule," *infra*. Justices Stevens and Ginsburg dissented from the grant of qualified immunity.

[361] 480 U.S. 709 (1987).

[362] 480 U.S. at 725. Not at issue was whether there must be individualized suspicion for investigations of work-related misconduct.

[363] This position was stated in Justice O'Connor's plurality opinion, joined by Chief Justice Rehnquist and by Justices White and Powell.

[364] 480 U.S. at 732 (Scalia, J., concurring in judgment).

[365] 560 U.S. ___, No. 08–1332, slip op. (2010).

[366] In *Quon*, a police officer was dismissed after a review of the transcripts of his on-duty text messages revealed that a large majority of his texting was not related to work, and some messages were sexually explicit.

[367] 560 U.S. ___, No. 08–1332, slip op. at 13 (2010).

rity."[368] So saying, the Court, in *Florence v. Board of Chosen Freeholders*, upheld routine strip searches, including close-up visual cavity inspections, as part of processing new arrestees for entry into the general inmate population, without the need for individualized suspicion and without an exception for those arrested for minor offenses.[369] Correctional officials had asserted significant penological interests to justify routine strip searches of new arrivals: detecting and preventing the introduction into the inmate population of infections, infestations, and contraband of all sorts; and identifying gang members. Having cited serious concerns and having applied their professional expertise, the officials had, in the Court's opinion, acted reasonably and not clearly overreacted. But despite taking a deferential approach and recounting the grave dangers correctional officers face, the Florence Court did not hold that individuals being processed for detention have no privacy rights at all. In separate concurrences, moreover, two members of the five-Justice majority held out the prospect of exceptions and refinements in future rulings on blanket strip search policies for new detainees.[370]

The Court in *Maryland v. King* cited a legitimate interest in having safe and accurate booking procedures to identify persons being taken into custody in order to sustain taking DNA samples from those charged with serious crimes.[371] Tapping the "unmatched potential of DNA identification" facilitates knowing with certainty who the arrestee is, the arrestee's criminal history, the danger the arrestee poses to others, the arrestee's flight risk, and other relevant facts.[372] By comparison, the Court characterized an arrestee's expectation of privacy as diminished and the intrusion posed by a cheek swab as minimal.[373]

Searches of prison cells by prison administrators are not limited even by a reasonableness standard, the Court's having held that "the Fourth Amendment proscription against unreasonable searches

[368] Florence v. Board of Chosen Freeholders, 566 U.S. ___, No. 10–945, slip op. at 2, 9 (2012). *See also, e.g.,* Bell v. Wolfish, 441 U.S. 520 (1979). The Florence Court made clear it was referring to "jails" in "a broad sense to include prisons and other detention facilities." 566 U.S. ___, No. 10–945, slip op. at 1 (2012).

[369] 566 U.S. ___, No. 10–945, slip op. (2012). The Court upheld similarly invasive strip searches of all inmates following contact visits in Bell v. Wolfish. 441 U.S. 520, 558–60 (1979).

[370] 566 U.S. ___, No. 10–945, slip op. (2012) (Roberts, C.J., concurring); 566 U.S. ___, No. 10–945, slip op. (2012) (Alito, J., concurring). In the opinion of the dissenters, a strip search of the kind conducted in Florence is unconstitutional if given to an arriving detainee arrested for a minor offense not involving violence or drugs, absent a reasonable suspicion to believe that the new arrival possesses contraband. 566 U.S. ___, No. 10–945, slip op. (2012) (Breyer, J., dissenting).

[371] 569 U.S. ___, No. 12–207, slip op. (2013).

[372] *Id.* at 10–18, 23.

[373] *Id.* at 23–26.

does not apply within the confines of the prison cell." [374] Thus, prison administrators may conduct random "shakedown" searches of inmates' cells without the need to adopt any established practice or plan, and inmates must look to the Eighth Amendment or to state tort law for redress against harassment, malicious property destruction, and the like.

Neither a warrant nor probable cause is needed for an administrative search of a probationer's home. It is enough, the Court ruled in *Griffin v. Wisconsin*, that such a search was conducted pursuant to a valid regulation that itself satisfies the Fourth Amendment's reasonableness standard (*e.g.*, by requiring "reasonable grounds" for a search). [375] "A State's operation of a probation system, like its operation of a school, government office or prison, or its supervision of a regulated industry, . . . presents 'special needs' beyond normal law enforcement that may justify departures from the usual warrant and probable cause requirements." [376] "Probation, like incarceration, is a form of criminal sanction," the Court noted, and a warrant or probable cause requirement would interfere with the "ongoing [non-adversarial] supervisory relationship" required for proper functioning of the system. [377] A warrant is also not required if the purpose of a search of a probationer is investigate a crime rather than to supervise probation. [378]

"[O]n the 'continuum' of state-imposed punishments . . . , parolees have [even] fewer expectations of privacy than probationers, because parole is more akin to imprisonment than probation is to imprisonment." [379] The Fourth Amendment, therefore, is not violated by a warrantless search of a parolee that is predicated upon a parole condition to which a prisoner agreed to observe during the balance of his sentence. [380]

Drug Testing.—In two 1989 decisions the Court held that no warrant, probable cause, or even individualized suspicion is re-

---

[374] Hudson v. Palmer, 468 U.S. 517, 526 (1984). *See also* Bell v. Wolfish, 441 U.S. 520, 555–57 (1979) ("It is difficult to see how the detainee's interest in privacy is infringed by the room-search rule [allowing unannounced searches]. No one can rationally doubt that room searches represent an appropriate security measure . . . .").

[375] 483 U.S. 868 (1987) (search based on information from police detective that there was or might be contraband in probationer's apartment).

[376] 483 U.S. at 873–74.

[377] 483 U.S. at 879.

[378] United States v. Knights, 534 U.S. 112 (2001) (probationary status informs both sides of the reasonableness balance).

[379] Samson v. California, 547 U.S. 843, 850 (2006) (internal quotation marks altered).

[380] 547 U.S. at 852. The parole condition at issue in *Samson* required prisoners to "agree in writing to be subject to a search or seizure by a parole officer or other peace officer at any time of the day or night, with or without a search warrant and with or without cause." Id. at 846, quoting Cal. Penal Code Ann. § 3067(a).

quired for mandatory drug testing of certain classes of railroad and public employees. In each case, "special needs beyond the normal need for law enforcement" were identified as justifying the drug testing. In *Skinner v. Railway Labor Executives' Ass'n*,[381] the Court upheld regulations requiring railroads to administer blood, urine, and breath tests to employees involved in certain train accidents or violating certain safety rules; in *National Treasury Employees Union v. Von Raab*[382] the Court upheld a Customs Service screening program requiring urine testing of employees seeking transfer or promotion to positions having direct involvement with drug interdiction, or to positions requiring the incumbent to carry firearms.

The Court in *Skinner* found a "compelling" governmental interest in testing the railroad employees without any showing of individualized suspicion, since operation of trains by anyone impaired by drugs "can cause great human loss before any signs of impairment become noticeable."[383] By contrast, the intrusions on privacy were termed "limited." Blood and breath tests were passed off as routine; the urine test, although more intrusive, was deemed permissible because of the "diminished expectation of privacy" in employees having some responsibility for safety in a pervasively regulated industry.[384] The lower court's emphasis on the limited effectiveness of the urine test (it detects past drug use but not necessarily the level of impairment) was misplaced, the Court ruled. It is enough that the test may provide some useful information for an accident investigation; in addition, the test may promote deterrence as well as detection of drug use.[385]

In *Von Raab* the governmental interests underlying the Customs Service's screening program were also termed "compelling": to ensure that persons entrusted with a firearm and the possible use of deadly force not suffer from drug-induced impairment of perception and judgment, and that "front-line [drug] interdiction personnel [be] physically fit, and have unimpeachable integrity and judgment."[386] The possibly "substantial" interference with privacy interests of these Customs employees was justified, the Court concluded, be-

---

[381] 489 U.S. 602 (1989).

[382] 489 U.S. 656 (1989).

[383] 489 U.S. at 628.

[384] 489 U.S. at 628.

[385] 489 U.S. at 631–32.

[386] *Von Raab*, 489 U.S. at 670–71. Dissenting Justice Scalia discounted the "feeble justifications" relied upon by the Court, believing instead that the "only plausible explanation" for the drug testing program was the "symbolism" of a government agency setting an example for other employers to follow. 489 U.S. at 686–87.

cause, "[u]nlike most private citizens or government employees generally, they have a diminished expectation of privacy." [387]

Emphasizing the "special needs" of the public school context, reflected in the "custodial and tutelary" power that schools exercise over students, and also noting schoolchildren's diminished expectation of privacy, the Court in *Vernonia School District v. Acton* [388] upheld a school district's policy authorizing random urinalysis drug testing of students who participate in interscholastic athletics. The Court redefined the term "compelling" governmental interest. The phrase does not describe a "fixed, minimum quantum of governmental concern," the Court explained, but rather "describes an interest which appears *important enough* to justify the particular search at hand." [389] Applying this standard, the Court concluded that "deterring drug use by our Nation's schoolchildren is at least as important as enhancing efficient enforcement of the Nation's laws against the importation of drugs . . . or deterring drug use by engineers and trainmen." [390] On the other hand, the interference with privacy interests was not great, the Court decided, since schoolchildren are routinely required to submit to various physical examinations and vaccinations. Moreover, "[l]egitimate privacy expectations are even less [for] student athletes, since they normally suit up, shower, and dress in locker rooms that afford no privacy, and since they voluntarily subject themselves to physical exams and other regulations above and beyond those imposed on non-athletes." [391] The Court "caution[ed] against the assumption that suspicionless drug testing will readily pass muster in other contexts," identifying as "the most significant element" in *Vernonia* the fact that the policy was implemented under the government's responsibilities as guardian and tutor of schoolchildren. [392]

Seven years later, the Court in *Board of Education v. Earls* [393] extended *Vernonia* to uphold a school system's drug testing of all junior high and high school students who participated in extracurricular activities. The lowered expectation of privacy that athletes have "was not essential" to the decision in *Vernonia*, Justice Thomas wrote for a 5–4 Court majority. [394] Rather, that decision "depended primarily upon the school's custodial responsibility and au-

---

[387] 489 U.S. at 672.
[388] 515 U.S. 646 (1995).
[389] 515 U.S. at 661.
[390] 515 U.S. at 661.
[391] 515 U.S. at 657.
[392] 515 U.S. at 665.
[393] 536 U.S. 822 (2002).
[394] 536 U.S. at 831.

thority."[395] Another distinction was that, although there was some evidence of drug use among the district's students, there was no evidence of a significant problem, as there had been in *Vernonia*. Rather, the Court referred to "the nationwide epidemic of drug use," and stated that there is no "threshold level" of drug use that need be present.[396] Because the students subjected to testing in *Earls* had the choice of not participating in extra-curricular activities rather than submitting to drug testing, the case stops short of holding that public school authorities may test all junior and senior high school students for drugs. Thus, although the Court's rationale seems broad enough to permit across-the-board testing,[397] Justice Breyer's concurrence, emphasizing among other points that "the testing program avoids subjecting the entire school to testing,"[398] raises some doubt on this score. The Court also left another basis for limiting the ruling's sweep by asserting that "regulation of extracurricular activities further diminishes the expectation of privacy among schoolchildren."[399]

In two other cases, the Court found that there were no "special needs" justifying random testing. Georgia's requirement that candidates for state office certify that they had passed a drug test, the Court ruled in *Chandler v. Miller*[400] was "symbolic" rather than "special." There was nothing in the record to indicate any actual fear or suspicion of drug use by state officials, the required certification was not well designed to detect illegal drug use, and candidates for state office, unlike the customs officers held subject to drug testing in *Von Raab*, are subject to "relentless" public scrutiny. In the second case, a city-run hospital's program for drug screening of preg-

[395] 536 U.S. at 831.
[396] 536 U.S. at 836.
[397] Drug testing was said to be a "reasonable" means of protecting the school board's "important interest in preventing and deterring drug use among its students," and the decision in *Vernonia* was said to depend "primarily upon the school's custodial responsibility and authority." 536 U.S. at 838, 831.
[398] Concurring Justice Breyer pointed out that the testing program "preserves an option for a conscientious objector," who can pay a price of nonparticipation that is "serious, but less severe than expulsion." 536 U.S. at 841. Dissenting Justice Ginsburg pointed out that extracurricular activities are "part of the school's educational program" even though they are in a sense "voluntary." "Voluntary participation in athletics has a distinctly different dimension" because it "expose[s] students to physical risks that schools have a duty to mitigate." Id. at 845, 846.
[399] 536 U.S. at 831–32. The best the Court could do to support this statement was to assert that "some of these clubs and activities require occasional off-campus travel and communal undress," to point out that all extracurricular activities "have their own rules and requirements," and to quote from general language in *Vernonia*. Id. Dissenting Justice Ginsburg pointed out that these situations requiring a change of clothes on occasional out-of-town trips are "hardly equivalent to the routine communal undress associated with athletics." Id. at 848.
[400] 520 U.S. 305 (1997).

nant patients suspected of cocaine use was invalidated because its purpose was to collect evidence for law enforcement.[401] In the previous three cases in which random testing had been upheld, the Court pointed out, the "special needs" asserted as justification were "divorced from the general interest in law enforcement."[402] By contrast, the screening program's focus on law enforcement brought it squarely within the Fourth Amendment's restrictions.

Electronic Surveillance and the Fourth Amendment

The Olmstead Case.—With the invention of the microphone, the telephone, and the dictagraph recorder, it became possible to "eavesdrop" with much greater secrecy and expediency. Inevitably, the use of electronic devices in law enforcement was challenged, and in 1928 the Court reviewed convictions obtained on the basis of evidence gained through taps on telephone wires in violation of state law. On a five-to-four vote, the Court held that wiretapping was not within the confines of the Fourth Amendment.[403] Chief Justice Taft, writing the opinion of the Court, relied on two lines of argument for the conclusion. First, because the Amendment was designed to protect one's property interest in his premises, there was no search so long as there was no physical trespass on premises owned or controlled by a defendant. Second, all the evidence obtained had been secured by hearing, and the interception of a conversation could not qualify as a seizure, for the Amendment referred only to the seizure of tangible items. Furthermore, the violation of state law did not render the evidence excludable, since the exclusionary rule operated only on evidence seized in violation of the Constitution.[404]

Federal Communications Act.—Six years after the decision in *Olmstead*, Congress enacted the Federal Communications Act and included in § 605 of the Act a broadly worded proscription on which the Court seized to place some limitation upon governmental wire-

---

[401] Ferguson v. City of Charleston, 532 U.S. 67 (2001).

[402] 532 U.S. at 79.

[403] Olmstead v. United States, 277 U.S. 438 (1928).

[404] Among the dissenters were Justice Holmes, who characterized "illegal" wiretapping as "dirty business," 277 U.S. at 470, and Justice Brandeis, who contributed to his opinion the famous peroration about government as "the potent, the omnipresent, teacher" which "breeds contempt for law" among the people by its example. Id. at 485. More relevant here was his lengthy argument rejecting the premises of the majority, an argument which later became the law of the land. (1) "To protect [the right to be left alone], every unjustifiable intrusion by the Government upon the privacy of the individual, whatever the means employed, must be deemed a violation of the Fourth Amendment." Id. at 478. (2) "There is, in essence, no difference between the sealed letter and the private telephone message. . . . The evil incident to invasion of the privacy of the telephone is far greater than that involved in tampering with the mails. Whenever a telephone line is tapped, the privacy of the persons at both ends of the line is invaded and all conversations between them upon any subject . . . may be overheard." Id. at 475–76.

tapping.[405] Thus, in *Nardone v. United States*,[406] the Court held that wiretapping by federal officers could violate § 605 if the officers both intercepted and divulged the contents of the conversation they overheard, and that testimony in court would constitute a form of prohibited divulgence. Such evidence was therefore excluded, although wiretapping was not illegal under the Court's interpretation if the information was not used outside the governmental agency. Because § 605 applied to intrastate as well as interstate transmissions,[407] there was no question about the applicability of the ban to state police officers, but the Court declined to apply either the statute or the due process clause to require the exclusion of such evidence from state criminal trials.[408] State efforts to legalize wiretapping pursuant to court orders were held by the Court to be precluded by the fact that Congress in § 605 had intended to occupy the field completely to the exclusion of the states.[409]

Nontelephonic Electronic Surveillance.—The trespass rationale of *Olmstead* was used in cases dealing with "bugging" of premises rather than with tapping of telephones. Thus, in *Goldman v. United States*,[410] the Court found no Fourth Amendment violation when a listening device was placed against a party wall so that conversations were overheard on the other side. But when officers drove a "spike mike" into a party wall until it came into contact with a heating duct and thus broadcast defendant's conversations, the Court determined that the trespass brought the case within the Amend-

---

[405] Ch. 652, 48 Stat. 1103 (1934), providing, inter alia, that ". . . no person not being authorized by the sender shall intercept any communication and divulge or publish the existence, contents, purport, effect, or meaning of such intercepted communication to any person." Nothing in the legislative history indicated what Congress had in mind in including this language. The section, which appeared at 47 U.S.C. § 605, was rewritten by Title III of the Omnibus Crime Act of 1968, 82 Stat. 22, § 803, so that the "regulation of the interception of wire or oral communications in the future is to be governed by" the provisions of Title III. S. REP. No. 1097, 90th Cong., 2d Sess. 107–08 (1968).

[406] 302 U.S. 379 (1937). Derivative evidence, that is, evidence discovered as a result of information obtained through a wiretap, was similarly inadmissible, Nardone v. United States, 308 U.S. 338 (1939), although the testimony of witnesses might be obtained through the exploitation of wiretap information. Goldstein v. United States, 316 U.S. 114 (1942). Eavesdropping on a conversation on an extension telephone with the consent of one of the parties did not violate the statute. Rathbun v. United States, 355 U.S. 107 (1957).

[407] Weiss v. United States, 308 U.S. 321 (1939).

[408] Schwartz v. Texas, 344 U.S. 199 (1952). At this time, evidence obtained in violation of the Fourth Amendment could be admitted in state courts. Wolf v. Colorado, 338 U.S. 25 (1949). Although *Wolf* was overruled by Mapp v. Ohio, 367 U.S. 643 (1961), it was some seven years later and after wiretapping itself had been made subject to the Fourth Amendment that *Schwartz* was overruled in Lee v. Florida, 392 U.S. 378 (1968).

[409] Bananti v. United States, 355 U.S. 96 (1957).

[410] 316 U.S. 129 (1942).

ment.[411] In so holding, the Court, without alluding to the matter, overruled in effect the second rationale of *Olmstead*, the premise that conversations could not be seized.

The Berger and Katz Cases.—In *Berger v. New York*,[412] the Court confirmed the obsolescence of the alternative holding in *Olmstead* that conversations could not be seized in the Fourth Amendment sense.[413] *Berger* held unconstitutional on its face a state eavesdropping statute under which judges were authorized to issue warrants permitting police officers to trespass on private premises to install listening devices. The warrants were to be issued upon a showing of "reasonable ground to believe that evidence of crime may be thus obtained, and particularly describing the person or persons whose communications, conversations or discussions are to be overheard or recorded." For the five-Justice majority, Justice Clark discerned several constitutional defects in the law. "First, . . . eavesdropping is authorized without requiring belief that any particular offense has been or is being committed; nor that the 'property' sought, the conversations, be particularly described."

"The purpose of the probable-cause requirement of the Fourth Amendment to keep the state out of constitutionally protected areas until it has reason to believe that a specific crime has been or is being committed is thereby wholly aborted. Likewise the statute's failure to describe with particularity the conversations sought gives the officer a roving commission to 'seize' any and all conversations. It is true that the statute requires the naming of 'the person or persons whose communications, conversations or discussions are to be overheard or recorded. . . .' But this does no more than identify the person whose constitutionally protected area is to be invaded rather than 'particularly describing' the communications, conversations, or discussions to be seized. . . . Secondly, authorization of eavesdropping for a two-month period is the equivalent of a series of intrusions, searches, and seizures pursuant to a single showing of probable cause. Prompt execution is also avoided. During such a long and continuous (24 hours a day) period the conversations of any and all persons coming into the area covered by the device will be seized indiscriminately and without regard to their connection with the crime under investigation. Moreover, the statute permits . . . extensions of the original two-month period—presumably for two months each—on a mere showing that such extension is 'in the

---

[411] Silverman v. United States, 365 U.S. 505 (1961). *See also* Clinton v. Virginia, 377 U.S. 158 (1964) (physical trespass found with regard to amplifying device stuck in a partition wall with a thumb tack).

[412] 388 U.S. 41 (1967).

[413] 388 U.S. at 50–53.

public interest.' . . . Third, the statute places no termination date on the eavesdrop once the conversation sought is seized. . . . Finally, the statute's procedure, necessarily because its success depends on secrecy, has no requirement for notice as do conventional warrants, nor does it overcome this defect by requiring some showing of special facts. On the contrary, it permits unconsented entry without any showing of exigent circumstances. Such a showing of exigency, in order to avoid notice, would appear more important in eavesdropping, with its inherent dangers, than that required when conventional procedures of search and seizure are utilized. Nor does the statute provide for a return on the warrant thereby leaving full discretion in the officer as to the use of seized conversations of innocent as well as guilty parties. In short, the statute's blanket grant of permission to eavesdrop is without adequate judicial supervision or protective procedures." [414]

Both Justices Black and White in dissent accused the *Berger* majority of so construing the Fourth Amendment that no wiretapping-eavesdropping statute could pass constitutional scrutiny,[415] and, in *Katz v. United States*,[416] the Court in an opinion by one of the *Berger* dissenters, Justice Stewart, modified some of its language and pointed to Court approval of some types of statutorily-authorized electronic surveillance. Just as *Berger* had confirmed that one rationale of the *Olmstead* decision, the inapplicability of "seizure" to conversations, was no longer valid, *Katz* disposed of the other rationale. In the latter case, officers had affixed a listening device to the outside wall of a telephone booth regularly used by Katz and activated it each time he entered; since there had been no physical trespass into the booth, the lower courts held the Fourth Amendment not relevant. The Court disagreed, saying that "once it is recognized that the Fourth Amendment protects people—and not simply 'areas'—against unreasonable searches and seizures, it becomes clear that the reach of that Amendment cannot turn upon the presence or absence of a physical intrusion into any given enclosure." [417] Because the surveillance

---

[414] 388 U.S. at 58–60. Justice Stewart concurred because he thought that the affidavits in this case had not been sufficient to show probable cause, but he thought the statute constitutional in compliance with the Fourth Amendment. Id. at 68. Justice Black dissented, arguing that the Fourth Amendment was not applicable to electronic eavesdropping but that in any event the "search" authorized by the statute was reasonable. Id. at 70. Justice Harlan dissented, arguing that the statute with its judicial gloss was in compliance with the Fourth Amendment. Id. at 89. Justice White thought both the statute and its application in this case were constitutional. Id. at 107.

[415] 388 U.S. at 71, 113.

[416] 389 U.S. 347 (1967).

[417] 389 U.S. at 353. "We conclude that the underpinnings of *Olmstead* and *Goldman* have been so eroded by our subsequent decisions that the 'trespass' doctrine

of Katz's telephone calls had not been authorized by a magistrate, it was invalid; however, the Court thought that "it is clear that this surveillance was so narrowly circumscribed that a duly authorized magistrate, properly notified of the need for such investigation, specifically informed of the basis on which it was to proceed, and clearly apprised of the precise intrusion it would entail, could constitutionally have authorized, with appropriate safeguards, the very limited search and seizure that the government asserts in fact took place."[418] The notice requirement, which had loomed in *Berger* as an obstacle to successful electronic surveillance, was summarily disposed of.[419] Finally, Justice Stewart observed that it was unlikely that electronic surveillance would ever come under any of the established exceptions so that it could be conducted without prior judicial approval.[420]

Following *Katz*, Congress enacted in 1968 a comprehensive statute authorizing federal officers and permitting state officers pursuant to state legislation complying with the federal law to seek warrants for electronic surveillance to investigate violations of prescribed

there enunciated can no longer be regarded as controlling. The Government's activities in electronically listening to and recording the petitioner's words violated the privacy upon which he justifiably relied while using the telephone booth and thus constituted a 'search and seizure' within the meaning of the Fourth Amendment."

[418] 389 U.S. at 354. The "narrowly circumscribed" nature of the surveillance was made clear by the Court in the immediately preceding passage. "[The Government agents] did not begin their electronic surveillance until investigation of the petitioner's activities had established a strong probability that he was using the telephone in question to transmit gambling information to persons in other States, in violation of federal law. Moreover, the surveillance was limited, both in scope and in duration, to the specific purpose of establishing the contents of the petitioner's unlawful telephonic communications. The agents confined their surveillance to the brief periods during which he used the telephone booth, and they took great care to overhear only the conversations of the petitioner himself." Id. For similar emphasis upon precision and narrow circumscription, *see* Osborn v. United States, 385 U.S. 323, 329–30 (1966).

[419] "A conventional warrant ordinarily serves to notify the suspect of an intended search . . . . In omitting any requirement of advance notice, the federal court . . . simply recognized, as has this Court, that officers need not announce their purpose before conducting an otherwise authorized search if such an announcement would provoke the escape of the suspect or the destruction of critical evidence." 389 U.S. at 355 n.16.

[420] 389 U.S. at 357–58. Justice Black dissented, feeling that the Fourth Amendment applied only to searches for and seizures of tangible things and not conversations. Id. at 364. Two "beeper" decisions support the general applicability of the warrant requirement if electronic surveillance will impair legitimate privacy interests. *Compare* United States v. Knotts, 460 U.S. 276 (1983) (no Fourth Amendment violation in relying on a beeper, installed without warrant, to aid in monitoring progress of a car on the public roads, since there is no legitimate expectation of privacy in destination of travel on the public roads), *with* United States v. Karo, 468 U.S. 705 (1984) (beeper installed without a warrant may not be used to obtain information as to the continuing presence of an item within a private residence).

classes of criminal legislation.[421] The Court has not yet had occasion to pass on the federal statute and to determine whether its procedures and authorizations comport with the standards sketched in *Osborn*, *Berger*, and *Katz* or whether those standards are somewhat more flexible than they appear to be on the faces of the opinions.[422]

Warrantless "National Security" Electronic Surveillance.—In *Katz v. United States*,[423] Justice White sought to preserve for a future case the possibility that in "national security cases" electronic surveillance upon the authorization of the President or the Attorney General could be permissible without prior judicial approval. The Executive Branch then asserted the power to wiretap and to "bug" in two types of national security situations, against domestic subversion and against foreign intelligence operations, first basing its authority on a theory of "inherent" presidential power and then in the Supreme Court withdrawing to the argument that such surveillance was a "reasonable" search and seizure and therefore valid under the Fourth Amendment. Unanimously, the Court held that at least in cases of domestic subversive investigations, compliance with the warrant provisions of the Fourth Amendment was required.[424] Whether or not a search was reasonable, wrote Justice Powell for the Court, was a question which derived much of its answer from the warrant clause; except in a few narrowly circumscribed classes of situations, only those searches conducted pursu-

---

[421] Title III of the Omnibus Crime Control and Safe Streets Act of 1968, 82 Stat. 211, 18 U.S.C. §§ 2510–20.

[422] The Court has interpreted the statute several times without reaching the constitutional questions. United States v. Kahn, 415 U.S. 143 (1974); United States v. Giordano, 416 U.S. 505 (1974); United States v. Chavez, 416 U.S. 562 (1974); United States v. Donovan, 429 U.S. 413 (1977); Scott v. United States, 436 U.S. 128 (1978); Dalia v. United States, 441 U.S. 238 (1979); United States v. New York Telephone Co., 434 U.S. 159 (1977); United States v. Caceres, 440 U.S. 741 (1979). *Dalia supra*, did pass on one constitutional issue, whether the Fourth Amendment mandated specific warrant authorization for a surreptitious entry to install an authorized "bug." *See also* Smith v. Maryland, 442 U.S. 735 (1979) (no reasonable expectation of privacy in numbers dialed on one's telephone, so Fourth Amendment does not require a warrant to install "pen register" to record those numbers).

[423] 389 U.S. 347, 363–64 (1967) (concurring opinion). Justices Douglas and Brennan rejected the suggestion. Id. at 359–60 (concurring opinion). When it enacted its 1968 electronic surveillance statute, Congress alluded to the problem in ambiguous fashion, 18 U.S.C. § 2511(3), which the Court subsequently interpreted as having expressed no congressional position at all. United States v. United States District Court, 407 U.S. 297, 302–08 (1972).

[424] United States v. United States District Court, 407 U.S. 297 (1972). Chief Justice Burger concurred in the result and Justice White concurred on the ground that the 1968 law required a warrant in this case, and therefore did not reach the constitutional issue. Id. at 340. Justice Rehnquist did not participate. Justice Powell carefully noted that the case required "no judgment on the scope of the President's surveillance power with respect to the activities of foreign powers, within or without this country." Id. at 308.

ant to warrants were reasonable. The Government's duty to preserve the national security did not override the guarantee that before government could invade the privacy of its citizens it must present to a neutral magistrate evidence sufficient to support issuance of a warrant authorizing that invasion of privacy.[425] This protection was even more needed in "national security cases" than in cases of "ordinary" crime, the Justice continued, because the tendency of government so often is to regard opponents of its policies as a threat and hence to tread in areas protected by the First Amendment as well as by the Fourth.[426] Rejected also was the argument that courts could not appreciate the intricacies of investigations in the area of national security or preserve the secrecy which is required.[427]

The question of the scope of the President's constitutional powers, if any, remains judicially unsettled.[428] Congress has acted, however, providing for a special court to hear requests for warrants for electronic surveillance in foreign intelligence situations, and permitting the President to authorize warrantless surveillance to acquire foreign intelligence information provided that the communications to be monitored are exclusively between or among foreign powers

---

[425] The case contains a clear suggestion that the Court would approve a congressional provision for a different standard of probable cause in national security cases. "We recognize that domestic security surveillance may involve different policy and practical considerations from the surveillance of 'ordinary crime.' The gathering of security intelligence is often long range and involves the interrelation of various sources and types of information. The exact targets of such surveillance may be more difficult to identify than in surveillance operations against many types of crimes specified in Title III. Often, too, the emphasis of domestic intelligence gathering is on the prevention of unlawful activity or the enhancement of the Government's preparedness for some future crisis or emergency. . . . Different standards may be compatible with the Fourth Amendment if they are reasonable both in relation to the legitimate need of Government for intelligence information and the protected rights of our citizens. For the warrant application may vary according to the governmental interest to be enforced and the nature of citizen right deserving protection. . . . It may be that Congress, for example, would judge that the application and affidavit showing probable cause need not follow the exact requirements of § 2518 but should allege other circumstances more appropriate to domestic security cases. . . ." 407 U.S. at 322–23.

[426] 407 U.S. at 313–24.

[427] 407 U.S. at 320.

[428] *See* United States v. Butenko, 494 F.2d 593 (3d Cir.), *cert. denied*, 419 U.S. 881 (1974); Zweibon v. Mitchell, 516 F.2d 594 (D.C. Cir. 1975), *cert. denied*, 425 U.S. 944 (1976), *appeal after remand*, 565 F.2d 742 (D.C. Cir. 1977), *on remand*, 444 F. Supp. 1296 (D.D.C. 1978), *aff'd in part, rev'd in part*, 606 F.2d 1172 (D.C. Cir. 1979), *cert. denied*, 453 U.S. 912 (1981); Smith v. Nixon, 606 F.2d 1183 (D.C. Cir. 1979), *cert. denied*, 453 U.S. 912 (1981); United States v. Truong Ding Hung, 629 F.2d 908 (4th Cir. 1980), after remand, 667 F.2d 1105 (4th Cir. 1981); Halkin v. Helms, 690 F.2d 977 (D.C. Cir. 1982).

and there is no substantial likelihood any "United States person" will be overheard.[429]

Enforcing the Fourth Amendment: The Exclusionary Rule

The Fourth Amendment declares a right to be free from unreasonable searches and seizures, but how this right translates into concrete terms is not specified. Several possible methods of enforcement have been suggested, but only one—the exclusionary rule—has been applied with any frequency by the Supreme Court, and Court in recent years has limited its application.

Alternatives to the Exclusionary Rule.—Theoretically, there are several alternatives to the exclusionary rule. An illegal search and seizure may be criminally actionable and officers undertaking one thus subject to prosecution, but the examples when officers are criminally prosecuted for overzealous law enforcement are extremely rare.[430] A police officer who makes an illegal search and seizure is subject to internal departmental discipline, which may be backed up by the oversight of police review boards in the few jurisdictions that have adopted them, but, again, the examples of disciplinary actions are exceedingly rare.[431]

Civil remedies are also available. Persons who have been illegally arrested or who have had their privacy invaded will usually have a tort action available under state statutory or common law, or against the Federal Government under the Federal Tort Claims Act.[432] Moreover, police officers acting under color of state law who violate a person's Fourth Amendment rights are subject to a suit in federal court for damages and other remedies[433] under a civil rights statute.[434] Although federal officers and others acting under color

---

[429] Foreign Intelligence Surveillance Act of 1978, Pub. L. 95–511, 92 Stat. 1797, 50 U.S.C. §§ 1801–1811. *See* United States v. Belfield, 692 F.2d 141 (D.C. Cir. 1982) (upholding constitutionality of disclosure restrictions in Act).

[430] Edwards, *Criminal Liability for Unreasonable Searches and Seizures*, 41 Va. L. Rev. 621 (1955).

[431] Goldstein, *Police Policy Formulation: A Proposal for Improving Police Performance*, 65 Mich. L. Rev. 1123 (1967).

[432] 28 U.S.C. §§ 1346(b), 2671–2680. Section 2680(h) prohibits suits against the Federal Government for false arrest and specified other intentional torts, but contains an exception "with regard to acts or omissions of investigative or law enforcement officials of the United States Government."

[433] If there are continuing and recurrent violations, federal injunctive relief would be available. *Cf.* Lankford v. Gelston, 364 F.2d 197 (4th Cir. 1966); Wheeler v. Goodman, 298 F. Supp. 935 (preliminary injunction), 306 F. Supp. 58 (permanent injunction) (W.D.N.C. 1969), *vacated on jurisdictional grounds*, 401 U.S. 987 (1971).

[434] 42 U.S.C. § 1983 (1964). *See* Monroe v. Pape, 365 U.S. 167 (1961). In some circumstances, the officer's liability may be attributed to the municipality. Monell v. New York City Dep't of Social Services, 436 U.S. 658 (1978). These claims that officers have used excessive force in the course of an arrest or investigatory stop are to be analyzed under the Fourth Amendment, not under substantive due process. The

of federal law are not subject to this statute, the Supreme Court has held that a right to damages for a violation of Fourth Amendment rights arises by implication and that this right is enforceable in federal courts.[435]

Although a damages remedy might be made more effectual,[436] legal and practical problems stand in the way.[437] Law enforcement officers have available to them the usual common-law defenses, the most important of which is the claim of good faith.[438] Such "good faith" claims, however, are not based on the subjective intent of the officer. Instead, officers are entitled to qualified immunity "where clearly established law does not show that the search violated the Fourth Amendment,"[439] or where they had an objectively reasonable belief that a warrantless search later determined to violate the Fourth Amendment was supported by probable cause or exigent circumstances.[440] On the practical side, persons subjected to illegal ar-

test is "whether the officers' actions are 'objectively reasonable' under the facts and circumstances confronting them." Graham v. Connor, 490 U.S. 386, 397 (1989) (cited with approval in Scott v. Harris, 550 U.S. 372, 381 (2007), in which a police officer's ramming a fleeing motorist's car from behind in an attempt to stop him was found reasonable).

[435] Bivens v. Six Unknown Named Agents, 403 U.S. 388 (1971). The possibility had been hinted at in Bell v. Hood, 327 U.S. 678 (1946).

[436] *See, e.g.*, Chief Justice Burger's dissent in Bivens v. Six Unknown Fed. Narcotics Agents, 403 U.S. 388, 411, 422–24 (1971), which suggests a statute allowing suit against the government in a special tribunal and a statutory remedy in lieu of the exclusionary rule.

[437] Foote, *Tort Remedies for Police Violations of Individual Rights*, 39 Minn. L. Rev. 493 (1955).

[438] This is the rule in actions under 42 U.S.C. § 1983, Pierson v. Ray, 386 U.S. 547 (1967), and on remand in *Bivens* the court of appeals promulgated the same rule to govern trial of the action. Bivens v. Six Unknown Named Agents of the Federal Bureau of Narcotics, 456 F.2d 1339 (2d Cir. 1972).

[439] Pearson v. Callahan, 555 U.S. ___, No. 07–751, slip op. (2009), quoted in Safford Unified School District #1 v. Redding, 557 U.S. ___, No. 08–479, slip op. at 11 (2009). In Saucier v. Katz, 533 U.S. 194 (2001), the Court had mandated a two-step procedure to determine whether an officer has qualified immunity: first, a determination whether the officer's conduct violated a constitutional right, and then a determination whether the right had been clearly established. In *Pearson*, the Court held "that, while the sequence set forth [in *Saucier*] is often appropriate, it should no longer be regarded as mandatory. The judges of the district courts and the courts of appeals should be permitted to exercise their sound discretion in deciding which of the two prongs of the qualified immunity analysis should be addressed first in light of the circumstances in the particular case at hand." 555 U.S. ___, No. 07–751, slip op. at 10. *See also* Harlow v. Fitzgerald, 457 U.S. 800, 818 (1982).

[440] Anderson v. Creighton, 483 U.S. 635 (1987). The qualified immunity inquiry "has a further dimension" beyond what is required in determining whether a police officer used excessive force in arresting a suspect: the officer may make "a reasonable mistake" in his assessment of what the law requires. Saucier v. Katz, 533 U.S. 194, 205–06 (2001). *See also* Brosseau v. Haugen, 543 U.S. 194, 201 (2004) (because cases create a "hazy border between excessive and acceptable force," an officer's misunderstanding as to her authority to shoot a suspect attempting to flee in a vehicle was not unreasonable); Malley v. Briggs, 475 U.S. 335, 345 (1986) (qualified immu-

rests and searches and seizures are often disreputable persons toward whom juries are unsympathetic, or they are indigent and unable to sue. The result, therefore, is that the Court has emphasized exclusion of unconstitutionally seized evidence in subsequent criminal trials as the only effective enforcement method.

Development of the Exclusionary Rule.—Exclusion of evidence as a remedy for Fourth Amendment violations found its beginning in *Boyd v. United States*,[441] which, as noted above, involved not a search and seizure but a compulsory production of business papers, which the Court likened to a search and seizure. Further, the Court analogized the Fifth Amendment's self-incrimination provision to the Fourth Amendment's protections to derive a rule that required exclusion of the compelled evidence because the defendant had been compelled to incriminate himself by producing it.[442] *Boyd* was closely limited to its facts and an exclusionary rule based on Fourth Amendment violations was rejected by the Court a few years later, with the Justices adhering to the common-law rule that evidence was admissible however acquired.[443]

Nevertheless, ten years later the common-law view was itself rejected and an exclusionary rule propounded in *Weeks v. United*

---

nity protects police officers who applied for a warrant unless "a reasonably well-trained officer in [the same] position would have known that his affidavit failed to establish probable cause and that he should not have applied for a warrant"). *But see* Mullenix v. Luna, 577 U.S. ___, No. 14–1143, slip op. at 8 (2015) (per curiam) ("The Court has . . . never found the use of deadly force in connection with a dangerous car chase to violate the Fourth Amendment, let alone be the basis for denying qualified immunity.").

[441] 116 U.S. 616 (1886).

[442] "We have already noticed the intimate relation between the two Amendments. They throw great light on each other. For the 'unreasonable searches and seizures' condemned in the Fourth Amendment are almost always made for the purpose of compelling a man to give evidence against himself, which in criminal cases is condemned in the Fifth Amendment; and compelling a man in a criminal case to be a witness against himself, which is condemned in the Fifth Amendment, throws light on the question as to what is an 'unreasonable search and seizure' within the meaning of the Fourth Amendment. And we have been unable to perceive that the seizure of a man's private books and papers to be used in evidence against him is substantially different from compelling him to be a witness against himself. We think it is within the clear intent and meaning of those terms." 116 U.S. at 633. It was this use of the Fifth Amendment's clearly required exclusionary rule, rather than one implied from the Fourth, on which Justice Black relied, and, absent a Fifth Amendment self-incrimination violation, he did not apply such a rule. Mapp v. Ohio, 367 U.S. 643, 661 (1961) (concurring opinion); Coolidge v. New Hampshire, 403 U.S. 443, 493, 496–500 (1971) (dissenting opinion). The theory of a "convergence" of the two Amendments has now been disavowed by the Court. *See* discussion, *supra*, under "Property Subject to Seizure."

[443] Adams v. New York, 192 U.S. 585 (1904). Since the case arose from a state court and concerned a search by state officers, it could have been decided simply by holding that the Fourth Amendment was inapplicable. *See* National Safe Deposit Co. v. Stead, 232 U.S. 58, 71 (1914).

States.[444] Weeks had been convicted on the basis of evidence seized from his home in the course of two warrantless searches; some of the evidence consisted of private papers such as those sought to be compelled in *Boyd*. Unanimously, the Court held that the evidence should have been excluded by the trial court. The Fourth Amendment, Justice Day said, placed on the courts as well as on law enforcement officers restraints on the exercise of power compatible with its guarantees. "The tendency of those who execute the criminal laws of the country to obtain convictions by means of unlawful searches and enforced confessions . . . should find no sanction in the judgments of the courts which are charged at all times with the support of the Constitution and to which people of all conditions have a right to appeal for the maintenance of such fundamental rights."[445] The basis of the ruling is ambiguous, but seems to have been an assumption that admission of illegally seized evidence would itself violate the Fourth Amendment. "If letters and private documents can thus be seized and held and used in evidence against a citizen accused of an offense, the protection of the Fourth Amendment declaring his right to be secured against such searches and seizures is of no value, and, so far as those thus placed are concerned, might as well be stricken from the Constitution. The efforts of the courts and their officials to bring the guilty to punishment, praiseworthy as they are, are not to be aided by the sacrifice of those great principles established by years of endeavor and suffering which have resulted in their embodiment in the fundamental law of the land."[446]

Because the Fourth Amendment does not restrict the actions of state officers,[447] there was originally no question about the application of an exclusionary rule in state courts[448] as a mandate of federal constitutional policy.[449] But, in *Wolf v. Colorado*,[450] a unanimous Court held that freedom from unreasonable searches and seizures

---

[444] 232 U.S. 383 (1914).

[445] 232 U.S. at 392.

[446] 232 U.S. at 393.

[447] Smith v. Maryland, 59 U.S. (18 How.) 71, 76 (1855); National Safe Deposit Co. v. Stead, 232 U.S. 58, 71 (1914).

[448] The history of the exclusionary rule in the state courts was surveyed by Justice Frankfurter in Wolf v. Colorado, 338 U.S. 25, 29, 33–38 (1949). The matter was canvassed again in Elkins v. United States, 364 U.S. 206, 224–32 (1960).

[449] During the period in which the Constitution did not impose any restrictions on state searches and seizures, the Court permitted the introduction in evidence in federal courts of items seized by state officers which had they been seized by federal officers would have been inadmissible, Weeks v. United States, 232 U.S. 383, 398 (1914), so long as no federal officer participated in the search, Byars v. United States, 273 U.S. 28 (1927), or the search was not made on behalf of federal law enforcement purposes. Gambino v. United States, 275 U.S. 310 (1927). This rule became known as the "silver platter doctrine" after the phrase coined by Justice Frankfurter in Lustig v. United States, 338 U.S. 74, 78–79 (1949): "The crux of that doctrine is that a search is a search by a federal official if he had a hand in it; it is not

was such a fundamental right as to be protected against state violations by the Due Process Clause of the Fourteenth Amendment.[451] However, the Court held that the right thus guaranteed did not require that the exclusionary rule be applied in the state courts, because there were other means to observe and enforce the right. "Granting that in practice the exclusion of evidence may be an effective way of deterring unreasonable searches, it is not for this Court to condemn as falling below the minimal standards assured by the Due Process Clause a State's reliance upon other methods which, if consistently enforced, would be equally effective." [452]

It developed, however, that the Court had not vested in the states total discretion with regard to the admissibility of evidence, as the Court proceeded to evaluate under the due process clause the methods by which the evidence had been obtained. Thus, in *Rochin v. California*,[453] evidence of narcotics possession had been obtained by forcible administration of an emetic to defendant at a hospital after officers had been unsuccessful in preventing him from swallowing certain capsules. The evidence, said Justice Frankfurter for the Court, should have been excluded because the police methods were too objectionable. "This is conduct that shocks the conscience. Illegally breaking into the privacy of the petitioner, the struggle to open his mouth and remove what was there, the forcible extraction of his stomach's contents . . . is bound to offend even hardened sensibilities. They are methods too close to the rack and screw." [454] The *Rochin* standard was limited in *Irvine v. California*,[455] in which defendant was convicted of bookmaking activities on the basis of evidence secured by police who repeatedly broke into his house and

a search by a federal official if evidence secured by state authorities is turned over to the federal authorities on a silver platter." In Elkins v. United States, 364 U.S. 206 (1960), the doctrine was discarded by a five-to-four majority, which held that, because Wolf v. Colorado, 338 U.S. 25 (1949), had made state searches and seizures subject to federal constitutional restrictions through the Fourteenth Amendment's due process clause, the "silver platter doctrine" was no longer constitutionally viable. During this same period, since state courts were free to admit any evidence no matter how obtained, evidence illegally seized by federal officers could be used in state courts, Wilson v. Schnettler, 365 U.S. 381 (1961), although the Supreme Court ruled out such a course if the evidence had first been offered in a federal trial and had been suppressed. Rea v. United States, 350 U.S. 214 (1956).

450 338 U.S. 25 (1949).

451 "The security of one's privacy against arbitrary intrusion by the police—which is at the core of the Fourth Amendment—is basic to a free society. It is therefore implicit in 'the concept of ordered liberty' and as such enforceable against the States through the Due Process Clause." 338 U.S. at 27–28.

452 338 U.S. at 31.

453 342 U.S. 165 (1952). The police had initially entered defendant's house without a warrant. Justices Black and Douglas concurred in the result on self-incrimination grounds.

454 342 U.S. at 172.

455 347 U.S. 128 (1954).

concealed electronic gear to broadcast every conversation in the house. Justice Jackson's plurality opinion asserted that *Rochin* had been occasioned by the element of brutality, and that while the police conduct in *Irvine* was blatantly illegal the admissibility of the evidence was governed by *Wolf,* which should be consistently applied for purposes of guidance to state courts. The Justice also entertained considerable doubts about the efficacy of the exclusionary rule.[456] *Rochin* emerged as the standard, however, in a later case in which the Court sustained the admissibility of the results of a blood test administered while defendant was unconscious in a hospital following a traffic accident, the Court observing the routine nature of the test and the minimal intrusion into bodily privacy.[457]

Then, in *Mapp v. Ohio,*[458] the Court held that the exclusionary rule applied to the states. It was "logically and constitutionally necessary," wrote Justice Clark for the majority, "that the exclusion doctrine—an essential part of the right to privacy—be also insisted upon as an essential ingredient of the right" to be secure from unreasonable searches and seizures. "To hold otherwise is to grant the right but in reality to withhold its privilege and enjoyment." [459] The Court further held that, because illegally seized evidence was to be excluded from both federal and state courts, the standards by which the question of legality was to be determined should be the same, regardless of whether the court in which the evidence was offered was state or federal.[460]

The Foundations of the Exclusionary Rule.—Important to determination of such questions as the application of the exclusionary rule to the states and the ability of Congress to abolish or to limit it is the fixing of the constitutional source and the basis of

---

[456] 347 U.S. at 134–38. Justice Clark, concurring, announced his intention to vote to apply the exclusionary rule to the states when the votes were available. Id. at 138. Justices Black and Douglas dissented on self-incrimination grounds, id. at 139, and Justice Douglas continued to urge the application of the exclusionary rule to the states. Id. at 149. Justices Frankfurter and Burton dissented on due process grounds, arguing the relevance of *Rochin.* Id. at 142.

[457] Breithaupt v. Abram, 352 U.S. 432 (1957). Chief Justice Warren and Justices Black and Douglas dissented. Though a due process case, the results of the case have been reaffirmed directly in a Fourth Amendment case. Schmerber v. California, 384 U.S. 757 (1966).

[458] 367 U.S. 643 (1961).

[459] 367 U.S. at 655–56. Justice Black concurred, doubting that the Fourth Amendment itself compelled adoption of an exclusionary rule but relying on the Fifth Amendment for authority. Id. at 661. Justice Stewart would not have reached the issue but would have reversed on other grounds, id. at 672, while Justices Harlan, Frankfurter, and Whittaker dissented, preferring to adhere to *Wolf.* Id. at 672. Justice Harlan advocated the overruling of *Mapp* down to the conclusion of his service on the Court. *See* Coolidge v. New Hampshire, 403 U.S. 443, 490 (1971) (concurring opinion).

[460] Ker v. California, 374 U.S. 23 (1963).

the rule. For some time, it was not clear whether the exclusionary rule was derived from the Fourth Amendment, from some union of the Fourth and Fifth Amendments, or from the Court's supervisory power over the lower federal courts. It will be recalled that in *Boyd* [461] the Court fused the search and seizure clause with the provision of the Fifth Amendment protecting against compelled self-incrimination. In *Weeks v. United States*,[462] though the Fifth Amendment was mentioned, the holding seemed clearly to be based on the Fourth Amendment. Nevertheless, in opinions following *Weeks* the Court clearly identified the basis for the exclusionary rule as the Self-Incrimination Clause of the Fifth Amendment.[463] Then, in *Mapp v. Ohio*,[464] the Court tied the rule strictly to the Fourth Amendment, finding exclusion of evidence seized in violation of the Amendment to be the "most important constitutional privilege" of the right to be free from unreasonable searches and seizures, finding that the rule was "an essential part of the right of privacy" protected by the Amendment.

"This Court has ever since [Weeks was decided in 1914] required of federal law officers a strict adherence to that command which this Court has held to be a clear, specific, and *constitutionally required*—even if judicially implied—deterrent safeguard without insistence upon which the Fourth Amendment would have been reduced to a 'form of words.' " [465] It was a necessary step in the application of the rule to the states to find that the rule was of constitutional origin rather than a result of an exercise of the Court's supervisory power over the lower federal courts, because the latter

---

[461] Boyd v. United States, 116 U.S. 616 (1886).

[462] 232 U.S. 383 (1914). Defendant's room had been searched and papers seized by officers acting without a warrant. "If letters and private documents can thus be seized and held and used in evidence against a citizen accused of an offense, the protection of the Fourth Amendment declaring his right to be secure against such searches and seizures is of no value, and, so far as those thus placed are concerned, might as well be stricken from the Constitution." Id. at 393.

[463] *E.g.*, Gouled v. United States, 255 U.S. 298, 306, 307 (1921); Amos v. United States, 255 U.S. 313, 316 (1921); Agnello v. United States, 269 U.S. 20, 33–34 (1925); McGuire v. United States, 273 U.S. 95, 99 (1927). In Olmstead v. United States, 277 U.S. 438, 462 (1928), Chief Justice Taft ascribed the rule both to the Fourth and the Fifth Amendments, while in dissent Justices Holmes and Brandeis took the view that the Fifth Amendment was violated by the admission of evidence seized in violation of the Fourth. Id. at 469, 478–79. Justice Black was the only modern proponent of this view. Mapp v. Ohio, 367 U.S. 643, 661 (1961) (concurring opinion); Coolidge v. New Hampshire, 403 U.S. 443, 493, 496–500 (1971) (dissenting opinion). *See*, however, Justice Clark's plurality opinion in Ker v. California, 374 U.S. 23, 30 (1963), in which he brought up the self-incrimination clause as a supplementary source of the rule, a position which he had discarded in *Mapp*.

[464] 367 U.S. 643, 656 (1961). Wolf v. Colorado, 338 U.S. 25, 28 (1949), also ascribed the rule to the Fourth Amendment exclusively.

[465] Mapp v. Ohio, 367 U.S. 643, 648 (1961) (emphasis added).

could not constitutionally be extended to the state courts.[466] In fact, in *Wolf v. Colorado*,[467] in declining to extend the exclusionary rule to the states, Justice Frankfurter seemed to find the rule to be based on the Court's supervisory powers. *Mapp* establishes that the rule is of constitutional origin, but this does not necessarily establish that it is immune to statutory revision.

Suggestions appear in a number of cases, including *Weeks*, to the effect that admission of illegally seized evidence is itself unconstitutional.[468] These suggestions were often combined with a rationale emphasizing "judicial integrity" as a reason to reject the proffer of such evidence.[469] Yet the Court permitted such evidence to be introduced into trial courts when the defendant lacked "standing" to object to the search and seizure that produced the evidence[470] or when the search took place before the announcement of the deci-

---

[466] An example of an exclusionary rule not based on constitutional grounds may be found in McNabb v. United States, 318 U.S. 332 (1943), and Mallory v. United States, 354 U.S. 449 (1957), in which the Court enforced a requirement that arrestees be promptly presented to a magistrate by holding that incriminating admissions obtained during the period beyond a reasonable time for presentation would be inadmissible. The rule was not extended to the States, *cf.* Culombe v. Connecticut, 367 U.S. 568, 598–602 (1961), but the Court's resort to the self-incrimination clause in reviewing confessions made such application irrelevant in most cases in any event. For an example of a transmutation of a supervisory rule into a constitutional rule, *see* McCarthy v. United States, 394 U.S. 459 (1969), and Boykin v. Alabama, 395 U.S. 238 (1969).

[467] *Weeks* "was not derived from the explicit requirements of the Fourth Amendment . . . . The decision was a matter of judicial implication." 338 U.S. 25, 28 (1949). Justice Black was more explicit. "I agree with what appears to be a plain implication of the Court's opinion that the federal exclusionary rule is not a command of the Fourth Amendment but is a judicially created rule of evidence which Congress might negate." Id. at 39–40. He continued to adhere to the supervisory power basis in strictly search-and-seizure cases, Berger v. New York, 388 U.S. 41, 76 (1967) (dissenting), except where self-incrimination values were present. Mapp v. Ohio, 367 U.S. 643, 661 (1961) (concurring). *See also* id. at 678 (Justice Harlan dissenting); Elkins v. United States, 364 U.S. 206, 216 (1960) (Justice Stewart for the Court).

[468] "The tendency of those who execute the criminal laws of the country to obtain convictions by means of unlawful searches and enforced confessions . . . should find no sanction in the judgment of the courts which are charged at all times with the support of the Constitution . . . ." Weeks v. United States, 232 U.S. 383, 392 (1914). In Mapp v. Ohio, 367 U.S. 643, 655, 657 (1961), Justice Clark maintained that "the Fourth Amendment include[s] the exclusion of the evidence seized in violation of its provisions" and that it, and the Fifth Amendment with regard to confessions "assures . . . that no man is to be convicted on unconstitutional evidence." In Terry v. Ohio, 392 U.S. 1, 12, 13 (1968), Chief Justice Warren wrote: "Courts which sit under our Constitution cannot and will not be made party to lawless invasions of the constitutional rights of citizens by permitting unhindered governmental use of the fruits of such invasions. . . . A ruling admitting evidence in a criminal trial . . . has the necessary effect of legitimizing the conduct which produced the evidence."

[469] Elkins v. United States, 364 U.S. 206, 222–23 (1960); Mapp v. Ohio, 367 U.S. 643, 660 (1961). *See* McNabb v. United States, 318 U.S. 332, 339–40 (1943).

[470] *See* "Operation of the Rule: Standing," *infra*.

sion extending the exclusionary rule to the states.[471] At these times, the Court turned to the "basic postulate of the exclusionary rule itself. The rule is calculated to prevent, not to repair. Its purpose is to deter—to compel respect for the constitutional guaranty in the only effectively available way—by removing the incentive to disregard it."[472] "*Mapp* had as its prime purpose the enforcement of the Fourth Amendment through the inclusion of the exclusionary rule within its rights. This, it was found, was the only effective deterrent to lawless police action. Indeed, all of the cases since *Wolf* requiring the exclusion of illegal evidence have been based on the necessity for an effective deterrent to illegal police action."[473]

Narrowing Application of the Exclusionary Rule.—For as long as we have had the exclusionary rule, critics have attacked it, challenged its premises, disputed its morality.[474] By the early 1980s, a majority of Justices had stated a desire either to abolish the rule or to sharply curtail its operation,[475] and numerous opinions had rejected all doctrinal bases other than deterrence.[476] At the same

---

[471] Linkletter v. Walker, 381 U.S. 618 (1965).

[472] Elkins v. United States, 364 U.S. 206, 217 (1960).

[473] Linkletter v. Walker, 381 U.S. 618, 636–37 (1965). The Court advanced other reasons for its decision as well. Id. at 636–40.

[474] Among the early critics were Judge Cardozo, People v. Defore, 242 N.Y. 13, 21, 150 N.E. 585, 587 (1926) (the criminal will go free "because the constable has blundered"), and Dean Wigmore. 8 J. Wigmore, A Treatise on the Anglo-American System of Evidence 2183–84 (3d ed. 1940). For extensive discussion of criticism and support, with citation to the literature, *see* 1 Wayne R. LaFave, Search and Seizure: A Treatise on the Fourth Amendment § 1.2 (4th ed. 2004).

[475] *E.g.*, Stone v. Powell, 428 U.S. 465, 496 (1976) (Chief Justice Burger: rule ought to be discarded now, rather than wait for a replacement as he argued earlier); id. at 536 (Justice White: modify rule to admit evidence seized illegally but in good faith); Schneckloth v. Bustamonte, 412 U.S. 218, 261 (1973) (Justice Powell); Brown v. Illinois, 422 U.S. 590, 609 (1975) (Justice Powell); Robbins v. California, 453 U.S. 420, 437 (1981) (Justice Rehnquist); California v. Minjares, 443 U.S. 916 (1979) (Justice Rehnquist, joined by Chief Justice Burger); Coolidge v. New Hampshire, 403 U.S. 443, 510 (1971) (Justice Blackmun joining Justice Black's dissent that "the Fourth Amendment supports no exclusionary rule").

[476] *E.g.*, United States v. Janis, 428 U.S. 433, 446 (1976) (deterrence is the "prime purpose" of the rule, "if not the sole one."); United States v. Calandra, 414 U.S. 338, 347–48 (1974); United States v. Peltier, 422 U.S. 531, 536–39 (1975); Stone v. Powell, 428 U.S. 465, 486 (1976); Rakas v. Illinois, 439 U.S. 128, 134 n.3, 137–38 (1978); Michigan v. DeFillippo, 443 U.S. 31, 38 n.3 (1979). Thus, admission of the fruits of an unlawful search or seizure "work[s] no new Fourth Amendment wrong," the wrong being "fully accomplished by the unlawful search or seizure itself," United States v. Calandra, 414 U.S. at 354, and the exclusionary rule does not "cure the invasion of the defendant's rights which he has already suffered." Stone v. Powell, 428 U.S. at 540 (Justice White dissenting). "Judicial integrity" is not infringed by the mere admission of evidence seized wrongfully. "[T]he courts must not commit or encourage violations of the Constitution," and the integrity issue is answered by whether exclusion would deter violations by others. United States v. Janis, 428 U.S. at 458 n.35; United States v. Calandra, 414 U.S. at 347, 354; United States v. Peltier, 422 U.S. at 538; Michigan v. Tucker, 417 U.S. 433, 450 n.25 (1974).

time, these opinions voiced strong doubts about the efficacy of the rule as a deterrent, and advanced public interest values in effective law enforcement and public safety as reasons to discard the rule altogether or curtail its application.[477] Thus, the Court emphasized the high costs of enforcing the rule to exclude reliable and trustworthy evidence, even when violations have been technical or in good faith, and suggested that such use of the rule may well "generat[e] disrespect for the law and administration of justice,"[478] as well as free guilty defendants.[479] No longer does the Court declare that "[t]he essence of a provision forbidding the acquisition of evidence in a certain way is that not merely evidence so acquired shall not be used before the Court but that it shall not be used at all."[480]

Although the exclusionary rule has not been completely repudiated, its use has been substantially curbed. For instance, defendants who themselves were not subjected to illegal searches and seizures may not object to the introduction of evidence illegally obtained from co-conspirators or codefendants,[481] and even a defendant whose rights have been infringed may find the evidence admitted, not as proof of guilt, but to impeach his testimony.[482] Further, evidence obtained through a wrongful search and seizure may sometimes be used directly in the criminal trial, if the prosecution can show a sufficient attenuation of the link between police misconduct and obtaining the evidence.[483] Defendants who have been convicted after trials in which they were given a full and fair opportu-

---

[477] United States v. Janis, 428 U.S. 433, 448–54 (1976), contains a lengthy review of the literature on the deterrent effect of the rule and doubts about that effect. *See also* Stone v. Powell, 428 U.S. 465, 492 n.32 (1976).

[478] Stone v. Powell, 428 U.S. at 490, 491.

[479] Bivens v. Six Unknown Fed. Narcotics Agents, 403 U.S. 388, 416 (1971) (Chief Justice Burger dissenting).

[480] Silverthorne Lumber Co. v. United States, 251 U.S. 385, 392 (1920).

[481] *E.g.*, Rakas v. Illinois, 439 U.S. 128 (1978); United States v. Padilla, 508 U.S. 77 (1993) (only persons whose privacy or property interests are violated may object to a search on Fourth Amendment grounds; exerting control and oversight over property by virtue of participation in a criminal conspiracy does not alone establish such interests); United States v. Salvucci, 448 U.S. 83 (1980); Rawlings v. Kentucky, 448 U.S. 98 (1980). In United States v. Payner, 447 U.S. 727 (1980), the Court held it impermissible for a federal court to exercise its supervisory power to police the administration of justice in the federal system to suppress otherwise admissible evidence on the ground that federal agents had flagrantly violated the Fourth Amendment rights of third parties in order to obtain evidence to use against others when the agents knew that the defendant would be unable to challenge their conduct under the Fourth Amendment.

[482] United States v. Havens, 446 U.S. 620 (1980); Walder v. United States, 347 U.S. 62 (1954). *Cf.* Agnello v. United States, 269 U.S. 20 (1925) (now vitiated by *Havens*). The impeachment exception applies only to the defendant's own testimony, and may not be extended to use illegally obtained evidence to impeach the testimony of other defense witnesses. James v. Illinois, 493 U.S. 307 (1990).

[483] Wong Sun v. United States, 371 U.S. 471, 487–88 (1963); Alderman v. United States, 394 U.S. 165, 180–85 (1969); Brown v. Illinois, 422 U.S. 590 (1975); Taylor v.

nity to raise claims of Fourth Amendment violations may not subsequently raise those claims on federal habeas corpus because, the Court found, the costs outweigh the minimal deterrent effect.[484]

The exclusionary rule is inapplicable in parole revocation hearings,[485] and a violation of the "knock-and-announce" rule (the procedure that police officers must follow to announce their presence before entering a residence with a lawful warrant)[486] does not require suppression of the evidence gathered pursuant to a search.[487] If an arrest or a search that was valid at the time it took place becomes bad through the subsequent invalidation of the statute under which the arrest or search was made, the Court has held that evidence obtained thereby is nonetheless admissible.[488] In other cases,

---

Alabama, 457 U.S. 687 (1982); Utah v. Strieff, 579 U.S. ___, No. 14–1373, slip op. (2016). United States v. Ceccolini, 435 U.S. 268 (1978), refused to exclude the testimony of a witness discovered through an illegal search. Because a witness was freely willing to testify and therefore more likely to come forward, the application of the exclusionary rule was not to be tested by the standard applied to exclusion of inanimate objects. Deterrence would be little served and relevant and material evidence would be lost to the prosecution. In New York v. Harris, 495 U.S. 14 (1990), the Court refused to exclude a station-house confession made by a suspect whose arrest at his home had violated the Fourth Amendment because, even though probable cause had existed, no warrant had been obtained. And, in Segura v. United States, 468 U.S. 796 (1984), evidence seized pursuant to a warrant obtained after an illegal entry was admitted because there had been an independent basis for issuance of the warrant. This rule also applies to evidence observed in plain view during the initial illegal search. Murray v. United States, 487 U.S. 533 (1988). *See also* United States v. Karo, 468 U.S. 705 (1984) (excluding consideration of tainted evidence, there was sufficient untainted evidence in affidavit to justify finding of probable cause and issuance of search warrant).

[484] Stone v. Powell, 428 U.S. 465, 494 (1976).

[485] Pennsylvania Bd. of Probation and Parole v. Scott, 524 U.S. 357 (1998).

[486] The "knock and announce" requirement is codified at 18 U.S.C. § 3109, and the Court has held that the rule is also part of the Fourth Amendment reasonableness inquiry. Wilson v. Arkansas, 514 U.S. 927 (1995).

[487] Hudson v. Michigan, 547 U.S. 586 (2006). Writing for the majority, Justice Scalia explained that the exclusionary rule was inappropriate because the purpose of the knock-and-announce requirement was to protect human life, property, and the homeowner's privacy and dignity; the requirement has never protected an individual's interest in preventing seizure of evidence described in a warrant. Id. at 594. Furthermore, the Court believed that the "substantial social costs" of applying the exclusionary rule would outweigh the benefits of deterring knock-and-announce violations by applying it. Id. The Court also reasoned that other means of deterrence, such as civil remedies, were available and effective, and that police forces have become increasingly professional and respectful of constitutional rights in the past half-century. Id. at 599. Justice Kennedy wrote a concurring opinion emphasizing that "the continued operation of the exclusionary rule . . . is not in doubt." Id. at 603. In dissent, Justice Breyer asserted that the majority's decision "weakens, perhaps destroys, much of the practical value of the Constitution's knock-and-announce protection." Id. at 605.

[488] Michigan v. DeFillippo, 443 U.S. 31 (1979) (statute creating substantive criminal offense). Statutes that authorize unconstitutional searches and seizures but which have not yet been voided at the time of the search or seizure may not create this effect, however, Torres v. Puerto Rico, 442 U.S. 465 (1979); Ybarra v. Illinois, 444

a grand jury witness was required to answer questions even though the questions were based on evidence obtained from an unlawful search and seizure,[489] and federal tax authorities were permitted in a civil proceeding to use evidence that had been unconstitutionally seized from a defendant by state authorities.[490]

A significant curtailment of the exclusionary rule came in 1984 with the adoption of a "good faith" exception. In *United States v. Leon*,[491] the Court created an exception for evidence obtained as a result of officers' objective, good-faith reliance on a warrant, later found to be defective, issued by a detached and neutral magistrate. Justice White's opinion for the Court could find little benefit in applying the exclusionary rule where there has been good-faith reliance on an invalid warrant. Thus, there was nothing to offset the "substantial social costs exacted by the [rule]."[492] "The exclusionary rule is designed to deter police misconduct rather than to punish the errors of judges and magistrates," and in any event the Court considered it unlikely that the rule could have much deterrent effect on the actions of truly neutral magistrates.[493] Moreover, the Court thought that the rule should not be applied "to deter objectively reasonable law enforcement activity," and that "[p]enalizing the officer for the magistrate's error . . . cannot logically contribute to the deterrence of Fourth Amendment violations."[494] The Court also suggested some circumstances in which courts would be unable to find that officers' reliance on a warrant was objectively reasonable: if the officers have been "dishonest or reckless in preparing their affidavit," if it should have been obvious that the magistrate had "wholly abandoned" his neutral role, or if the warrant was obviously deficient on its face (*e.g.*, lacking in particularity).

U.S. 85 (1979). This aspect of *Torres* and *Ybarra* was to a large degree nullified by Illinois v. Krull, 480 U.S. 340 (1987), rejecting a distinction between substantive and procedural statutes and holding the exclusionary rule inapplicable in the case of a police officer's objectively reasonable reliance on a statute later held to violate the Fourth Amendment. Similarly, the exclusionary rule does not require suppression of evidence that was seized incident to an arrest that was the result of a clerical error by a court clerk. Arizona v. Evans, 514 U.S. 1 (1995).

[489] United States v. Calandra, 414 U.S. 338 (1974).

[490] United States v. Janis, 428 U.S. 433 (1976). Similarly, the rule is inapplicable in civil proceedings for deportation of aliens. INS v. Lopez-Mendoza, 468 U.S. 1032 (1984).

[491] 468 U.S. 897 (1984). The same objectively reasonable "good-faith" rule now applies in determining whether officers obtaining warrants are entitled to qualified immunity from suit. Malley v. Briggs, 475 U.S. 335 (1986).

[492] 468 U.S. at 907.

[493] 468 U.S. at 916–17.

[494] 468 U.S. at 919, 921.

The Court applied the *Leon* standard in *Massachusetts v. Sheppard*,[495] holding that an officer possessed an objectively reasonable belief that he had a valid warrant after he had pointed out to the magistrate that he had not used the standard form, and the magistrate had indicated that the necessary changes had been incorporated in the issued warrant. Then, the Court then extended *Leon* to hold that the exclusionary rule is inapplicable to evidence obtained by an officer acting in objectively reasonable reliance on a statute later held to violate the Fourth Amendment.[496] Justice Blackmun's opinion for the Court reasoned that application of the exclusionary rule in such circumstances would have no more deterrent effect on officers than it would when officers reasonably rely on an invalid warrant, and no more deterrent effect on legislators who enact invalid statutes than on magistrates who issue invalid warrants.[497] Finally, the Court has held that the exclusionary rule does not apply if the police conduct a search in objectively reasonable reliance on binding judicial precedent, even a defendant successfully challenges that precedent.[498]

The Court also applied *Leon* to allow the admission of evidence obtained incident to an arrest that was based on a mistaken belief that there was probable cause to arrest, where the mistaken belief had resulted from a negligent bookkeeping error by a police employee other than the arresting officer. In *Herring v. United States*,[499] a police employee had failed to remove from the police computer database an arrest warrant that had been recalled five months earlier, and the arresting officer as a consequence mistakenly believed that the arrest warrant remained in effect. The Court upheld the

---

[495] 468 U.S. 981 (1984).

[496] Illinois v. Krull, 480 U.S. 340 (1987). The same difficult-to-establish qualifications apply: there can be no objectively reasonable reliance "if, in passing the statute, the legislature wholly abandoned its responsibility to enact constitutional laws," or if "a reasonable officer should have known that the statute was unconstitutional." Id. at 355.

[497] Dissenting Justice O'Connor disagreed with this second conclusion, suggesting that the grace period "during which the police may freely perform unreasonable searches . . . creates a positive incentive [for legislatures] to promulgate unconstitutional laws," and that the Court's ruling "destroys all incentive on the part of individual criminal defendants to litigate the violation of their Fourth Amendment rights" and thereby obtain a ruling on the validity of the statute. 480 U.S. at 366, 369.

[498] Davis v. United States, 564 U.S. ___, No. 09–11328, slip op. (2011). Justice Breyer, in dissent, points out that under Griffith v. Kentucky, 479 U.S. 314 (1987), "a new rule for the conduct of criminal prosecutions is to be applied retroactively to all cases, state or federal, pending on direct review or not yet final . . . ." Thus, the majority opinion in Davis would allow the incongruous result that a defendant could prove his Fourth Amendment rights had been violated, but could still be left without a viable remedy. Id. at 2 (Breyer, J., dissenting).

[499] 555 U.S. ___, No. 07–513, slip op. (2009), *Herring* was a five-to-four decision, with two dissenting opinions.

admission of evidence because the error had been "the result of iso- lated negligence attenuated from the arrest." [500] Although the Court did "not suggest that all recordkeeping errors by the police are im- mune from the exclusionary rule," it emphasized that, "[t]o trigger the exclusionary rule, police conduct must be sufficiently deliberate that exclusion can meaningfully deter it, and sufficiently culpable that such deterrence is worth the price paid by the justice system. As laid out in our cases, the exclusionary rule serves to deter delib- erate, reckless, or grossly negligent conduct, or in some circum- stances recurring or systemic negligence." [501]

Herring is significant because previous cases applying the good- faith exception to the exclusionary rule have involved principally Fourth Amendment violations not by the police, but by other gov- ernmental entities, such as the judiciary or the legislature. Al- though the error in *Herring* was committed by a police employee other than the arresting officer, the introduction of a balancing test to evaluate police conduct raises the possibility that even Fourth Amendment violations caused by the negligent actions of an arrest- ing officer might in the future evade the application of the exclusion- ary rule.[502]

For instance, it is unclear from the Court's analysis in *Leon* and its progeny whether a majority of the Justices would also support a good-faith exception for evidence seized without a warrant, al- though there is some language broad enough to apply to warrant- less seizures.[503] It is also unclear what a good-faith exception would

---

[500] 129 S. Ct. at 698.

[501] 129 S. Ct. at 703, 702. Justice Ginsburg, in a dissent joined by Justices Ste- vens, Souter, and Breyer, stated that "the Court's opinion underestimates the need for a forceful exclusionary rule and the gravity of recordkeeping errors in law en- forcement." Id. at 706. Justice Ginsburg added that the majority's suggestion that the exclusionary rule "is capable of only marginal deterrence when the misconduct at issue is merely careless, not intentional or reckless . . . runs counter to a founda- tional premise of tort law—that liability for negligence, *i.e.*, lack of due care, creates an incentive to act with greater care." Id. at 708. Justice Breyer, in a dissent joined by Justice Souter, noted that, although the Court had previously held that recordkeep- ing errors made by a court clerk do not trigger the exclusionary rule, Arizona v. Evans, 514 U.S. 1 (1995), he believed that recordkeeping errors made by the police should trigger the rule, as the majority's "case-by-case, multifactored inquiry into the degree of police culpability" would be difficult for the courts to administer. Id. at 711.

[502] *See Leon*, 468 U.S. 897, 926 (1984) (articulating, in *dicta*, an "intentional or reckless" misconduct standard for obviating "good faith" reliance on an invalid war- rant).

[503] The thrust of the analysis in *Leon* was with the reasonableness of reliance on a warrant. The Court several times, however, used language broad enough to apply to warrantless searches as well. *See, e.g.*, 468 U.S. at 909 (quoting Justice White's concurrence in Illinois v. Gates): "the balancing approach that has evolved . . . 'forcefully suggest[s] that the exclusionary rule be more generally modified to permit the introduction of evidence obtained in the reasonable good-faith belief that

mean in the context of a warrantless search, because the objective reasonableness of an officer's action in proceeding without a warrant is already taken into account in determining whether there has been a Fourth Amendment violation.[504] The Court's increasing willingness to uphold warrantless searches as not "unreasonable" under the Fourth Amendment, however, may reduce the frequency with which the good-faith issue arises in the context of the exclusionary rule.[505]

Another significant curtailment of the exclusionary rule involves the attenuation exception, which permits the use of evidence discovered through the government's unconstitutional conduct if the "causal link" between that misconduct and the discovery of the evidence is seen by the reviewing courts as sufficiently remote or has been interrupted by some intervening circumstances.[506] In a series of decisions issued over several decades, the Court has invoked this exception in upholding the admission of challenged evidence. For example, in *Wong Sun v. United States*, the Court upheld the admission of an unsigned statement made by a defendant who initially had been unlawfully arrested because, thereafter, the defendant was lawfully arraigned, released on his own recognizance, and, only then, voluntarily returned several days later to make the unsigned statement.[507] Similarly, in its 1984 decision in *Segura v. United States*, the Court upheld the admission of evidence obtained following an illegal entry into a residence because the evidence was seized the next day pursuant to a valid search warrant that had been issued based on information obtained by law enforcement before the illegal entry.[508]

---

a search or seizure was in accord with the Fourth Amendment'"; and id. at 919: "[the rule] cannot be expected, and should not be applied, to deter objectively reasonable law enforcement activity."

[504] *See* Yale Kamisar, *Gates, 'Probable Cause', 'Good Faith', and Beyond*, 69 Iowa L. Rev. 551, 589 (1984) (imposition of a good-faith exception on top of the "already diluted" standard for validity of a warrant "would amount to double dilution").

[505] *See, e.g.*, Illinois v. Rodriguez, 497 U.S. 177 (1990) (upholding search premised on officer's reasonable but mistaken belief that a third party had common authority over premises and could consent to search); Schneckloth v. Bustamonte, 412 U.S. 218 (1973) (no requirement of knowing and intelligent waiver in consenting to warrantless search); New York v. Belton, 453 U.S. 454 (1981) (upholding warrantless search of entire interior of passenger car, including closed containers, as incident to arrest of driver); Arizona v. Gant, 556 U.S. ___, No. 07–542 (U.S. Apr. 21 (2009), slip op. at 18 (the *Belton* rule applies "only if the arrestee is within reaching distance of the passenger compartment at the time of the search or it is reasonable to believe that the vehicle contains evidence of the offense of arrest"); United States v. Ross, 456 U.S. 798 (1982) (upholding warrantless search of movable container found in a locked car trunk).

[506] Utah v. Strieff, 579 U.S. ___, No. 14–1373, slip op. at 5 (2016).

[507] 371 U.S. 471, 491 (1963).

[508] 468 U.S. 796, 813–16 (1984).

More recently, in its 2016 decision in *Utah v. Strieff*, the Court rejected a challenge to the admission of certain evidence obtained as the result of an unlawful stop on the grounds that the discovery of an arrest warrant after the stop attenuated the connection between the unlawful stop and the evidence seized incident to the defendant's arrest.[509] As a threshold matter, the Court rejected the state court's view that the attenuation exception applies only in cases involving "an independent act of a defendant's 'free will.' "[510] Instead, the Court relied on three factors it had set forth in a Fifth Amendment case, *Brown v. Illinois*,[511] to determine whether the subsequent lawful acquisition of evidence was sufficiently attenuated from the initial misconduct: (1) the "temporal proximity" between the two acts; (2) the presences of intervening circumstances; and (3) the purpose and flagrancy of the official misconduct.[512] On the whole, the *Strieff* Court, reiterating that "suppression of evidence should be the courts' "last resort, not our first impulse,"[513] concluded that the circumstances of the case weighed in favor of the admission of the challenged evidence. While the closeness in time between the initial stop and the search was seen by the Court as favoring suppression,[514] the presence of intervening circumstances in the form of a valid warrant for the defendant's arrest strongly favored the state,[515] and in the Court's view, there was no indication that this unlawful stop was part of any "systematic or recurrent police misconduct."[516] In particular, the Court, relying on the second factor, emphasized that the discovery of a warrant "broke the causal chain" between the unlawful stop and the discovery of the challenged evidence.[517] As such, the *Strieff* Court appeared to establish a rule that the existence of a valid warrant, "predat[ing the] investigation" and "entirely unconnected with the stop," gener-

---

[509] *Strieff*, slip op. at 1. The state in *Strieff* had conceded that law enforcement lacked reasonable suspicion for the stop, *id.* at 2, and the Supreme Court characterized the search of the defendant following his arrest as a lawful search incident to arrest, *id.* at 8.

[510] Id. at 5 (quoting State v. Strieff, 457 P.3d 532, 544 (Utah 2015)).

[511] *See* 422 U.S. 590, 603–04 (1970) (holding that the state supreme court in this case had erroneously concluded that *Miranda* warnings always served to purge the taint of an illegal arrest).

[512] *See Strieff*, slip op. at 6–9.

[513] *Id.* at 8 (quoting Hudson v. Michigan, 547 U.S. 586, 591 (2006) (internal quotations omitted)).

[514] *Id.* at 6 (noting that "only minutes" passed between the unlawful stop and the discovery of the challenged evidence).

[515] *Id.* at 6–7. The *Strieff* Court emphasized that it viewed the warrant as "compelling" the officer to arrest the suspect. *Id.* at 9; *see also id.* at 7 (similar).

[516] *Id.* at 8.

[517] *Id.* at 9.

ally favors finding sufficient attenuation between the unlawful conduct and the discovery of evidence.[518]

Operation of the Rule: Standing.—The Court for a long period followed a rule of "standing" by which it determined whether a party was the appropriate person to move to suppress allegedly illegal evidence. Akin to Article III justiciability principles, which emphasize that one may ordinarily contest only those government actions that harm him, the standing principle in Fourth Amendment cases "require[d] of one who seeks to challenge the legality of a search as the basis for suppressing relevant evidence that he allege, and if the allegation be disputed that he establish, that he himself was the victim of an invasion of privacy."[519] Subsequently, the Court departed from the concept of standing to telescope the inquiry into one inquiry rather than two. Finding that standing served no useful analytical purpose, the Court has held that the issue of exclusion is to be determined solely upon a resolution of the substantive question whether the claimant's Fourth Amendment rights have been violated. "We can think of no decided cases of this Court that would have come out differently had we concluded . . . that the type of standing requirement . . . reaffirmed today is more properly subsumed under substantive Fourth Amendment doctrine. Rigorous application of the principle that the rights secured by this Amendment are personal, in place of a notion of 'standing,' will produce no additional situations in which evidence must be excluded. The inquiry under either approach is the same."[520] One must therefore show that "the disputed search and seizure has infringed an interest of the defendant which the Fourth Amendment was designed to protect."[521]

The *Katz* reasonable expectation of privacy rationale has now displaced property-ownership concepts that previously might have supported either standing to suppress or the establishment of an interest that has been invaded. Thus, it is no longer sufficient to allege possession or ownership of seized goods to establish the interest, if a justifiable expectation of privacy of the defendant was not violated in the seizure.[522] Also, it is no longer sufficient that one merely be lawfully on the premises in order to be able to object

---

[518] *Id.* at 7.

[519] Jones v. United States, 362 U.S. 257, 261 (1960). That is, the movant must show that he was "a victim of search or seizure, one against whom the search was directed, as distinguished from one who claims prejudice only through the use of evidence gathered as a consequence of search or seizure directed at someone else." Id. *See* Alderman v. United States, 394 U.S. 165, 174 (1969).

[520] Rakas v. Illinois, 439 U.S. 128, 139 (1978).

[521] 439 U.S. at 140.

[522] Previously, when ownership or possession was the issue, such as a charge of possessing contraband, the Court accorded "automatic standing" to one on the basis,

to an illegal search; rather, one must show some legitimate interest in the premises that the search invaded.[523] The same illegal search might, therefore, invade the rights of one person and not of another.[524] Again, the effect of the application of the privacy rationale has been to narrow considerably the number of people who can complain of an unconstitutional search.

first, that to require him to assert ownership or possession at the suppression hearing would be to cause him to incriminate himself with testimony that could later be used against him, and, second, that the government could not simultaneously assert that defendant was in possession of the items and deny that it had invaded his interests. Jones v. United States, 362 U.S. 257, 261–65 (1960). *See also* United States v. Jeffers, 342 U.S. 48 (1951). In Simmons v. United States, 390 U.S. 377 (1968), however, the Court held inadmissible at the subsequent trial admissions made in suppression hearings. When it then held that possession alone was insufficient to give a defendant the interest to move to suppress, because he must show that the search itself invaded his interest, the second consideration was mooted as well, and thus the "automatic standing" rule was overturned. United States v. Salvucci, 448 U.S. 83 (1980) (stolen checks found in illegal search of apartment of the mother of the defendant, in which he had no interest; defendant could not move to suppress on the basis of the illegal search); Rawlings v. Kentucky, 448 U.S. 98 (1980) (drugs belonging to defendant discovered in illegal search of friend's purse, in which he had no privacy interest; admission of ownership insufficient to enable him to move to suppress).

[523] Rakas v. Illinois, 439 U.S. 128 (1978) (passengers in automobile had no privacy interest in interior of the car; could not object to illegal search). United States v. Padilla, 508 U.S. 77 (1993) (only persons whose privacy or property interests are violated may object to a search on Fourth Amendment grounds; exerting control and oversight over property by virtue of participation in a criminal conspiracy does not alone establish such interests). Jones v. United States, 362 U.S. 257 (1960), had established the rule that anyone legitimately on the premises could object; the rationale was discarded but the result in *Jones* was maintained because he was there with permission, he had his own key, his luggage was there, he had the right to exclude and therefore a legitimate expectation of privacy. Similarly maintained were the results in United States v. Jeffers, 342 U.S. 48 (1951) (hotel room rented by defendant's aunts to which he had a key and permission to store things); Mancusi v. DeForte, 392 U.S. 364 (1968) (defendant shared office with several others; though he had no reasonable expectation of absolute privacy, he could reasonably expect to be intruded on only by other occupants and not by police).

[524] *E.g.,* Rawlings v. Kentucky, 448 U.S. 98 (1980) (fearing imminent police search, defendant deposited drugs in companion's purse where they were discovered in course of illegal search; defendant had no legitimate expectation of privacy in her purse, so that *his* Fourth Amendment rights were not violated, although hers were).

Made in the USA
Las Vegas, NV
23 January 2021